MEDITATIONS ON A RUSSIAN MARTIAL ART

James Sommerville

Front Cover Design: Christopher Levesque

Copyright 2020 James Sommerville
All Rights Reserved

Table of Contents

INTRODUCTION	1
1. A WAY OF LIFE	10
2. TRADITIONS	20
3. FOUNDATIONS	38
4. KNOW YOURSELF	58
5. THE NERVOUS SYSTEM(A)	80
6. NATURAL MOVEMENT	104
7. COURAGE	127
CONCLUSION	144
ACKNOWLEDGEMENTS	147
ABOUT THE AUTHOR	148

Introduction

When I selected meditation for the title of this book, I had in mind the original sense of the word. *Meditatio,* in Latin, denoted thinking over and contemplating a thing. But it also connoted preparing for something or practicing something, like a custom or a habit.[1]

When writing about early Christian monastics' meditation on Scripture, historian Jean Leclercq informs us that

> "for the ancients, to meditate is to read a text and to learn it 'by heart' in the fullest sense of the expression, that is, with one's whole being: with the body, since the mouth pronounced it, with the memory which fixes it, with the intelligence with understands its meaning and with the will which desires to put it into practice."[2]

In ancient times, for pagans and for Christians (and for other faiths besides), meditation was an experience rather than merely a mental event. It was an attempt at self-transformation.

This book is an expression of my own meditations on Systema, the 'Russian Martial Art'. It tries to put into words my various thoughts at the same time that it strengthens my practice. My hope is that, by the end of this book, having explored in detail, warts and all, a number of the art's most important elements, I'll have become a better student of it.

Whether this is foolish or not remains to be seen.

---

[1] Mary Carruthers, *The Craft of Thought: Meditation, Rhetoric, and the Crafting of Images, 400-1200* (Cambridge University Press, 1998): 82, 106

[2] Jean Leclercq, *The Love of Learning and the Desire for God: A Study of Monastic Culture*, translated by Catharine Misrahi (Fordham University Press, 1961): 22

Because a project like this presents certain risks. As Foucault reminds us, *meditatio* involves "appropriating [a thought] and being so profoundly convinced of it that we both believe it to be true and can also repeat it constantly and immediately whenever the need or opportunity to do so arrives."[3] In other words, meditation, as understood by the ancients, is a potential vehicle for fanaticism.

Becoming a fanatic would be counter-productive for someone trying to remain objective. I want to look closely at Systema, and absorb it into myself, without falling into its worldview and discourse.

***

Okay, fine, so what am I talking about? What is Systema?

It is a martial arts training regimen developed in Russia but introduced to the world primarily in the city of Toronto, Ontario, Canada.

Other schools call themselves Systema, but this book is about "The System" of Mikhail Ryabko, a Russian ex-military officer who reportedly holds the rank of Colonel, and of Vladimir Vasiliev, a gifted student of Ryabko, who brought Systema to Canada at the close of the Cold War.

Systema has schools across North America, mostly in cities that can sustain niche martial arts. However, you can also find clubs of varying prestige in South America, Europe, Australia, the Middle East, and Japan. Few of these clubs, even when an instructor is skilled in the art, are particularly well-known in their regions. Systema will never pop to mind as quickly as Brazilian Jiu-Jitsu or Karate or Aikido or any of the other traditional martial arts which one thinks of when one says 'martial arts'. But these clubs are out there. They talk to one another. Attend seminars together. Share information. And love Systema. All without me.

---

[3] Michel Foucault, *The Hermeneutics of the Subject: Lectures at the College de France, 1981-1982*, translated by Graham Burchell (Palgrave Macmillan, 2001): 357

I am a Systema nobody.

I'm not an instructor. I'm not even particularly skilled.

So why should you care to follow along on my 'meditation'?

My training in Systema began in September of 2006, under the direction of Emmanuel Manolakakis, a long-time instructor under Vasiliev. I like to joke with my friend that I practice Manolakakis Systema rather than Ryabko Systema, although neither of us has any questions about Manny's debt to and enthusiasm for the art's founder.

I have never met Ryabko. I know him only from videos, interviews, and testimony. Nor do I have much to do with Vasiliev, despite my close proximity to his school. I've only attended two seminars at Systema Headquarters (as it's called): one that I forget the name of, held in a school gymnasium at about the same time that HQ released the *Contact, Impact, and Control* DVD (2007), and the second recorded in the *Breathing and Fear* DVD (2017).

That said, I've participated in numerous other events at Fight Club, the school owned and operated by Manolakakis. Topics have included enclosed spaces, 'live' blades, and firearms. I've even taught a class or two over the years. And, with an extensive academic background, I have the skills to express my opinion in ways that others perhaps do not.

Manny once remarked that a book like the one now in your hands would be my gift to Systema. However, this is in *no way* meant to say that he endorses or even agrees with my interpretations. The thoughts and opinions expressed here are my own.

I'm not a master, but I'm certainly not a novice. With over a decade of experience in Systema as of the time of this writing, I'm entitled to an opinion.

***

As a martial art, Systema focuses upon situational awareness, movement under stress, the use of conventional weapons, and working with multiple opponents. It is a self-defense art rather than a combat or tournament art. A typical class is likely to involve simple exercises such as push-ups, squats, and leg raises, but also complex interactive exercises designed to stretch and structure bodies. Sparring is limited to special occasions. Most of our martial exercises are relatively static in comparison to, say, boxing. Nonetheless, we do strike and kick one another, forgoing the use of gloves or pads.

Students of Systema practice getting hit, or, as we say, "practice getting comfortable with contact." Everything aims toward learning how to remain comfortable. The Systema-trained individual is meant to resemble a soldier who is calm under fire. And, like a soldier, views violence as a form of work. It should be something you can do, like mixing cement or plotting a graph—nothing to write home about.

One way that a student trains to be comfortable is through breathing exercises—combinations of long and short inhales and exhales, sometimes mixed with breath-holds, regularly performed while running or doing basic exercises. For example, doing five slow push-ups in a single, long inhale, five slow push-ups in a single, long exhale, and then five slow push-ups while holding your breath. In Systema, the exercises are designed to make you fight with yourself, to gain physical and emotional control over yourself.

A good example of this would be "taking punches." The student stands upright in as relaxed a manner as possible, unprotected. Then, without knowing quite when, they are punched in the stomach. Experienced students, and most instructors, can strike quite deep. The student who absorbs the strike is often, if not winded, shocked. Fear responses are activated in the body. And now the student who has been made profoundly uncomfortable must, through breathing and movement, return themselves to comfort.

Why do this? You might say that it is to increase your fight intelligence. Conflicts of any sort, be they physical or merely social, tend to activate a stress response in the body, which tends in turn to reduce your ability to receive information, producing tunnel vision. Learning how to stay calm and comfortable during conflict, so the thinking goes, allows you to retain your awareness, continue to move, and remain cognizant of other threats.

***

In his *Civilization and Its Discontents*, Freud wrote that each of us seeks happiness in two supporting ways: we strive to remove pain and unpleasant experiences and we work to promote strong feelings of pleasure. Because suffering is so common, happiness is episodic; one day happiness is here, the next day it is gone, another it is back again; others hurt us (or we hurt ourselves with others), our bodies decay and worry, nature assaults us regularly without warning.

In response, humanity has developed "techniques of living" meant to ward off the effects of suffering. Freud lists eleven: denial, techno-science, intoxication, the control of the "inner sources of our needs," mental and intellectual work, art and entertainment, asceticism, polyamorous love, beauty, religion, and neurotic illness. We turn our eyes from the world or we seek to harness its powers; we teach ourselves self-control or fall into books; we watch TV or try to live off the grid; we find love in bodies or love in souls; we turn to god or are overtaken by madness. In all these ways and more we try to escape or otherwise manage the forces which assail us.[4]

Systema is, among other things, a technique of living. It represents one of the many, many ways through which humanity has sought to free itself from suffering. It does not remove suffering by deadening us, but teaches us how to manage pain as we live in the world. Through various ethical practices conducted in an environment of simulated conflict, it attempts to teach the mind and body to regulate and maybe even lessen destabilizing emotional responses.

To borrow a distinction made by philosopher Scott Samuelson, we can say that Systema is a "face it" approach

---

[4] Sigmund Freud, *Civilization and its Discontents*, translated by David McLintock (Penguin Books, 2002): 15-22

to suffering rather than a "fix it" approach.[5] You are placed into a position that naturally produces fear and tension, and then gradually taught—through breathing, relaxation, and movement—to consciously stand with your fear and control your tension.

One of the additional aims of this book, besides expressing my own attitudes and evaluations of Systema, will be to describe my beloved hobby as both a martial art and a technique of living. In this way, I hope that my words will be of interest to a broader readership.

***

When I write about Ryabko and Vasiliev, the founders of Systema, I will draw upon the sizable library of audio-visual materials published in English by Systema Headquarters. I will also make use of English language interviews, testimonials, videos, and advertisements available to the public on the internet. Were it possible for me to do so, I would have also consulted the available Russian language materials. Sadly, however, I can neither speak nor read Russian. I admit that this is a huge deficiency in my research. To mitigate any damage my ignorance may cause, I have, whenever possible, drawn on the work of scholars fluent with Russian and familiar with the country's politics and history.

When writing about the larger community of instructors who have been certified by Ryabko and Vasiliev, I'll quote either from North Carolina instructor Glenn Murphy's *Systema for Life* podcast, in which Murphy interviews practitioners from around the globe, or from the collection of interviews edited by UK instructor Rob Poyton, entitled *Systema Voices* (2018).

I'll also be reading from the training manuals published out of Systema Headquarters. Of particular interest to me will be Konstantin Komarov's *Systema Manual* (2014). Komarov, who is said to hold the rank of Major in the Russian special police service, is a well-regarded instructor in his own right, often considered on par with Ryabko and Vasiliev. The

---

[5] Scott Samuelson, *Seven Ways of Looking at Pointless Suffering* (The University of Chicago Press, 2018): 7

Systema Manual is Komarov's attempt to get down onto the page a description and analysis of the art's training methods. It is, for someone like myself, an exciting resource. Very few practitioners of Systema have placed the art into an intelligible framework.

Of secondary interest will be the works co-written by Vasiliev and his long-time student Scott Meredith: *Let Every Breath...: Secrets of the Russian Breath Masters* (2006), *Strikes: Soul Meets Body* (2015), and *Edge: Secrets of the Russian Blade Masters* (2018). These works are, for the most part, training drills framed within enthusiastic descriptions of Ryabko's and Vasiliev's abilities. Nonetheless, they serve as an important resource for learning about how Systema practitioners view themselves and their art.

To that same end, I'll also be drawing on an early guidebook published back in 1997, entitled, appropriately enough, *The Russian System Guidebook*.

Otherwise I'll be making use of my own experiences with Systema at Fight Club in Toronto, drawing from online footage to the fullest extent possible. This will allow you, the reader, to verify what I have to say and give you a better sense of what in-class work looks like.

***

The first part of this book regards the historical context of Systema. Chapter One argues that Systema's core features, its approach to truth, ethics, and practice, derive incidentally from a pre-modern conception of what it meant to be a philosopher. Back then philosophy was a way of life directed towards the emulation of a chosen sage. It is the same with Systema, whose students direct themselves toward the examples of Ryabko and Vasiliev.

Having drawn a line from Systema's present into the deep past, Chapter Two seeks to complicate the story. The art, at its core, may be as old as the hills, but the elements which have been attached to that core—nationalist myth, physical culture, and popular religion—are distinctly modern, having all emerged in Russia in at least the nineteenth century.

Chapter Three continues with this line of thought, looking as closely as possible at the biographies and teachings of Ryabko and Vasiliev, using any and all available digital and print materials, attempting to describe the development of Systema from a combat-oriented martial art, to a breath-centred way of life, to a modern brand identity.

We then turn once again in Chapter Four to ancient history, looking at Systema's relationship with the Delphic commandment "know yourself." Systema makes extensive use of this commandment, even going so far as to identify the art itself with the quest for self-knowledge. After reviewing the history of interpretations of this maxim, the chapter tries to highlight what is unique in Systema's approach. It argues that, in the Russian Martial Art, the quest to know yourself is in fact an invitation to reform your body and its emotions so that you can attend without thought to the present moment.

The second part of this book seeks to describe the actual practice of Systema. Chapter Five argues first that the Russian Martial Art is best understood, not as a *martial* art, but rather as a very physical *performance* art, one that seeks to embed in the hearts and minds of its practitioners the feeling of living and being part of a specific drama and narrative. The chapter then goes on to posit that Systema's central narrative is derived indirectly, if not directly, from nineteenth-century European and Russian anxieties regarding the deleterious effects of modernity, and more specifically from the languages of neurasthenia and, later, stress.

Afterwards, Chapter Six seeks to compare and contrast Systema's martial arts practices with those of traditional and modern martial arts and to further highlight the dramatic elements of its methodology. It describes the purpose of the art's training methods and attempts to explain the meaning behind its various somatic codes. Following that, there is an evaluation of Systema's relationship with violence. The chapter then takes the reader into an average training session, attempting to give some life to the practice.

Finally, Chapter Seven explores the theme of courage in Systema, first defining it as a term within virtue ethics and then, through a close reading of Komarov's *Systema Manual*, explaining the process by which Systema's instructors, both in theory and practice, seek to imbue their students with a capacity to regulate pain and face fear.

Once that's done, I'll have said all that I have to say. It will then be up to the reader to consider where and how I erred. Some will likely dismiss this book because the author 'just doesn't really get it.' They will say that I have not correctly plumbed the depths of Systema. Others, building off that notion, will submit that I am unentitled to my opinions, having not sought an instructorship or a higher level of mastery. Still others, steeped in the ideology of Orthodox monasticism, will quote from Theophan the Recluse: "Why do we criticize others? Because we do not try to know ourselves."[6] They will say that I have filled my mind with theories but not used them to work on myself.

If someone doesn't think that I possess a high enough level of mastery to have earned my opinion, then I cannot argue with them. We'll agree to disagree. But to Theophan and his fellow travelers, I would offer a counter-quotation, this one from the Stoic Roman Emperor Marcus Aurelius: "...latching onto things and piercing through them, so we see what they really are. That's what we need to do all the time—all through our lives when things lay claim to our trust—to lay them bare and see how pointless they are, to strip away the legend that encrusts them."[7] When meditating on Systema has not helped me to improve my practice, it has helped me to take Systema apart and see it for what it is.

---

[6] Theophan the Recluse, in *The Art of Prayer: An Orthodox Anthology*, translated by E. Kadloubovsky and E.M. Palmer, edited by Timothy Ware (Faber and Faber, 1966): 224

[7] Marcus Aurelius, *Meditations*, translated by Gregory Hays (The Modern Library, 2003): 71

1. A Way of Life

It is very common for experienced practitioners of Systema to use the analogy of an 'operating system' when they try to describe what their art is and how it works. A computer is hardware, a physical object with specific properties. It can compute at a certain speed and retain a certain amount of information. An operating system is software, a program which organizes other bits of software into a functional whole. A good operating system allows hardware and software to perform complex calculations more efficiently, maximizing the abilities of the computer overall. So too, the story goes, with Systema and the human being.

This idea of Systema as a method for optimizing human beings can be heard in the words of Osakan instructor Ryo Onishi:

> "Systema changes you, like, your perception. So basically, it shapes, reshapes your reality to somewhere closer to how it is. But most of the cases we see things with coloured glasses or something; maybe too much tension or emotion or whatever; we can't see things as it is."[1]

You hear it also in a different way from Austin instructor Gene Smithson: Systema is "not a fighting system; it's a method of growing a better, more realized human being."[2]

The first notable feature of these quotations is that they both announce that Systema is transformative. It changes, it reshapes, it betters, and it realizes. Moreover, it is reality itself that is affected. Onishi claims that Systema changes perception and reshapes reality, while Smithson understands

---

[1] *Systema for Life Podcast*, Episode 13, featuring Ryo Onishi (December 30, 2017)
[2] *Systema for Life Podcast*, Episode 5, featuring Gene Smithson (November 20, 2017)

Systema as a method that 'grows' a fully understood or 'realized' human being.

However they say it, these men are of the opinion that Systema operates at a level deeper than mere combat.

Openly concealed in such an idea of Systema is a realist notion of truth. For one must infer from Onishi that he believes that there is a way that things *are* and from Smithson that there *is* an ideal form of human being towards which one ought to strive. In other words, certain philosophical dogmas, both epistemological and ethical, underpin their conceptions of the art.

What is more, reading closely, one gets the distinct impression that in order to access this truth and realize this way of being, the practitioner of Systema must work to eliminate or lessen the influence of things called 'tension' and 'emotion'.

Systema, like ancient philosophy, names a style of thought that involves a particular view of the world and of the perfect human being and also a method of attaining that view point and perfection. It is, to borrow a term from historian Pierre Hadot, a way of life.[3]

***

Readers familiar with philosophy in the West from the ancients up until the early modern era will immediately recognize the similarities between the above analysis of Systema and the various schools of philosophy that had been practiced for centuries prior to the so-called Cartesian moment.

The cluster of ideas which surrounded the concept of philosophy underwent a profound and lasting shift somewhere between the seventeenth-century writings of Descartes and the eighteenth-century reform of European universities. Where before that time, philosophers, broadly

---

[3] Pierre Hadot, *Philosophy as a Way of Life: Spiritual Exercises from Socrates to Foucault*, edited by Arnold Davidson (Blackwell Publishing, 1995): 57

understood to include schoolmen and clerics, had engaged in spiritual and ascetic exercises in order to attune their bodies and minds to universal truths, philosophy now became a method of inquiring into the limits of truth itself.[4] And while this new philosophy contributed to the development of secularism and to scientific methods, as well as to the legal and political theories which continue to be practiced in the West up to the present day, one still sees that something was lost in the transition to modernity.

Philosophy used to be a way of life and not an academic profession. If you were a philosopher back then, before the early modern period, if you were a lover after wisdom, then you *meant* it. You took your truth seriously, building your entire life, including your thoughts and imaginings, around it.

This comparison between Systema and ancient philosophy might at first glance appear to be a superficial one. After all, what does Systema have to do with philosophical thought? The ancients, very much unlike the founders of Systema, included argument and refutation as part of their way of life. Art, in order to be art, even if it were an art of living, required a consistent account of one's nature, and a precise accumulation of reasons for believing in that account.[5] Anyone who has read from the ancient Stoics, for instance, will immediately see differences between Systema's exclusive

---

[4] Michel Foucault, *The Hermeneutics of the Subject: Lectures at the College de France, 1981-1982*, translated by Graham Burchell (Palgrave Macmillan, 2001): 15. For an example of philosophy as a way of life in medieval universities, see Gilles Mongeau, *Embracing Wisdom: The Summa Theologiae as Spiritual Pedagogy* (PIMS, 2015). For how this notion survived into the seventeenth-century, see Matthew L. Jones, *The Good Life in the Scientific Revolution: Descartes, Pascal, Leibniz, and the Cultivation of Virtue* (University of Chicago Press, 2006).
We do not begin to see a shift in this tradition until the publishing of Jacob Brucker's *Historia critica philosophia* in 1740. See Leo Catana, "The Concept of 'System of Philosophy': The Case of Jacob Brucker's Historiography of Philosophy," *History and Theory*, Volume 44 (2005)
[5] Marcel van Ackeren, "Self-Knowledge in Later Stoicism," in *Self-Knowledge: A History*, edited by Ursula Renz (Oxford University Press, 2017): 61

concern with bodily practice and the ancient philosophers' complex understandings of epistemology, metaphysics, and ethical theory.

Systema does not teach one how to think like a philosopher thinks. To quote from critical theorist Peter Sloterdijk, the cardinal exercise of the philosopher is a "withdrawal exercise... an exercise in not-taking-up-a-position, an exercise in de-existentialization, an attempt at the art of suspending participation in life in the midst of life."[6] Or, as he puts it later, philosophy "creates an artificial autism that isolates the thinker and takes him to a special world of imperative connected ideas."[7] In layman's terms, the philosopher is trained and practiced at stepping outside of himself and placing his head in the clouds. Systema, which—among other things—seeks to limit thought in order to encourage a constant present-mindedness, is not a philosophy in the above sense.

Nonetheless, there are good reasons for taking the comparison seriously. Ancient philosophical schools, generally speaking, constituted their way of life through the practice of spiritual exercises.[8] These exercises included attention to the self, meditation on principles, and consistent daily practice.[9] They also demanded of and promised to students the attainment of self-knowledge.[10] Furthermore, their way of life was exemplified by a sage to whom students looked as a model of behaviour and action.[11] Systema shares all three of these characteristics with the ancient schools.

Attention meant being attentive to yourself, watching yourself, examining yourself, cataloguing and evaluating

---

[6] Peter Sloterdijk, *The Art of Philosophy: Wisdom as Practice*, translated by Karen Margolis (Columbia University Press, 2012): 18
[7] *Ibid*: 29
[8] Pierre Hadot, *What Is Ancient Philosophy?*, translated by Michael Chase (Harvard University Press, 1995): 179-233.
[9] Hadot, *Philosophy as a Way of Life*: 85-86
[10] Ackeren, "Self-Knowledge in Later Stoicism": 62
[11] Rene Brouwer, "Sagehood and the Stoics," in *Oxford Studies in Ancient Philosophy*, Vol. 23, edited by David Sedley (Oxford University Press, 2002): 185

your habits and actions. Through such self-surveillance, it was said, you would be able to alter your way of being in the world.[12] In watching yourself, you could see whether the dogmas which you had accepted as true were truly being lived. For instance, if you believed that nature was cruel and beyond human control, and that emotional attachment to natural events was pointless, you needed also to see yourself living these ideas, controlling your outbursts, remaining impassive to misfortune, and treating others with justice and kindness.[13]

There are numerous examples of this sort of self-reflection in the practice of Systema. One day at Fight Club, just to pick an example, myself and another student were selected to perform an exercise in front of the class. It was a typical pushing drill, where partners go back and forth exchanging open-handed or closed-fist pushes to various parts of the body. As the class watched, Manny spoke, going over the various questions that one could ask of the performance. Were our feet moving enough? How was our distance? Were we being creative in the moment? Were we being precise? Did we have a rhythm? He then expanded those questions outward, encouraging the audience—including the performers—to ask larger questions: why were we here to train? Were we being good partners to each other?

It is in questions such as these, and in Manny's frequent instruction that we stay "half with ourselves and half with our partners," that I hear an echo of the ancient philosophers. Like them, Systema teaches self-reflection on the present moment. It asks: does your work stand up? Does it reflect your definition of the good?

Such attention to the present naturally contributes to acts of meditation.

For the ancients, meditation meant memorizing and assimilating the central ideas and tenants held by members of a philosophical school. It meant learning how to *think* like a Platonist, or a Stoic, or—later—a Christian. The aim, one

---

[12] Hadot, *Philosophy as a Way of Life*: 59
[13] Hadot, *What is Ancient Philosophy?*: 199-202

might say, if we are to continue with the metaphor of a computer's operating system, is to remove the old operating system and install a completely new one, to fundamentally re-program your way of perceiving the world and its inhabitants.

Indeed, one of the signs that Systema has taken hold as an operating system is that the practitioner begins to express genuine thoughts reminiscent of the opening lines of Epictetus' *Enchiridion*. The ancient Stoic manual reads:

> "Some things in the world are up to us, while others are not. Up to us are our faculties of judgement, motivation, desire, and aversion—in short, everything that is our own doing. Not up to us are our body and property, our reputations, and our official positions—in short, everything that is not our own doing."[14]

There will be time in later chapters to expand on the theme of Stoicism in Systema's way of life, so it is enough for now to state that, as in the above quote, Systema makes a distinction between what is yours, what is up to you, and what is not yours, what is not up to you.

What is up to you is your psychological state, how you judge, what you desire, what keeps you going, what pushes you away. Outside of such things, you do not get to make choices. You may become ill suddenly, there may be a flood; someone may start a rumour about you on the internet or someone else may get a promotion ahead of you. These material events can play havoc with your psyche, Systema maintains, *if you allow them to*.

But this distinction between the internal-ours and the external-not-ours does not tell the full story. In Systema's martial arts training, as well as in its general way of speaking, there is another important distinction which, again, the *Enchiridion* can help us to see. The manual reads: "Don't ask

---

[14] Epictetus, *How To Be Free: An Ancient Guide to the Stoic Life*, translated by A.A. Long (Princeton University Press, 2018): 3

for things to happen as you would like them to, but wish them to happen as they actually do, and you will be all right."[15]

Here you have a distinction made between your desired future and the experienced present. The goal of training, you might say, is to improve your ability to set aside your desire for future outcomes and accept that you will only ever receive the present moment as it happens to happen to you now. You are training, to put it another way, to go with the flow.

One manifestation of the above distinctions—between what is yours and what is not yours and between the desired future and the experienced present—is found in Systema's unique approach to combat, something that hasn't yet been described. Systema, unlike most other martial arts, does not practice set techniques. There are no katas, or arm bars, or kimuras, or round houses, or crane strikes, or anything else that is usually associated with martial practice. Yes, there is a core of exercises that are technique-like, but for the most part Systema is very free-form.

In class, Manny encourages us to "work from contact." What this means is to react to a grab or a strike not according to some imagined or desired future outcome but according to the experienced present. You don't know what something is going to *be* until it is actually happening, until it is present to you.

For example, when I see that someone is going to throw a kick at me, I could work prior to the arrival of the kick, which is possible and often warranted, or I could—if I wanted to be creative in that moment—let the kick connect, if even for a brief instant, in order to see what that kick *is*, not what I think it will be. From there, experiencing the kick in the present, the body can move and adapt according to the kick's force and direction.

Acting in this manner, we work to maintain the stability of our psyches, making sure to retain what is ours, that is, our judgements and desires, while accepting that we cannot

---
[15] *Ibid*: 17

control what is not ours, the events which occur to us. Sometimes a kick comes, we are struck, and we must adapt to a life of hard knocks, keeping always a calm and relaxed attitude.

Some ancients, the Stoics in particular, referred to this complex of attention, meditation, and practice as "the care of the self."[16] In caring for oneself, that is, in practicing to attend solely to the present moment, to articulate clearly the ideas of one's chosen school, and to take control of one's behaviour, the philosopher sought after wisdom, working to change the entirety of their life so that it more closely resembled the life of their ideal sage.

***

Each philosophical school had its ideal central figure. For Platonists, it was Plato; for Aristotelians, it was Aristotle; for the Cynics, it was Diogenes; for the Stoics, it was Zeno. And for all these schools, it was Socrates. In this figure of the sage, the ancients perceived someone who, through spiritual or philosophical ascent, had been set free from suffering yet still remained undoubtedly human.[17] He was tranquil and calm, performing with excellence his role in society, exhibiting a benevolent indifference to that which did not matter. He married, had a family, made money, and dealt with society as it came to him, without losing control of himself.[18]

The two sages of Systema are Ryabko and Vasiliev, about whom much more will be said in a later chapter. To the typical Systema instructor, the entire purpose of their involvement in the art is to bring their way of life as closely in line as possible with that of the founders. Again, Onishi's words are illustrative. When asked for words of advice to newcomers to Systema, he responds that you should seek immediately the presence of Ryabko and Vasiliev. Being in

---

[16] Michel Foucault, *The History of Sexuality, Part Two: The Use of Pleasure*, translated by Robert Hurley (Vintage, 1990): 73
[17] Hadot, *What is Ancient Philosophy?*: 223
[18] Julia Annas, "The Sage in Ancient Philosophy," in *Anthropine Sophia*, edited by F. Alesse (Bibliopolis 2008): 18-19

their presence is "like a shower you are taking," something that, just by virtue of emersion, cleanses your perception and alters your state of mind so that you perform better generally.[19]

This, perhaps, accounts for the anxiety that many experienced Systema instructors report feeling early on in their careers. They are acutely aware of the distance between their martial performance and that of their chosen masters. They want to *be like that*, but cannot. So instead they strive to live and teach according to the sages' principles.

Instructor Rob Poyton, when asked about his own large volume of instructional videos, responds that they are "basic, so yeah, what you see in, well, even pretty much now compared to what is achievable, it's all basic...I've always thought that my job, or the job of an instructor, is to be a signpost to people like Vladimir and Mikhail."[20]

Now, of course, it is not uncommon for individuals to have a role model. Most everyone has someone that they look up to. But with Systema, as with all philosophical ways of life, we are dealing with a relationship of greater intensity. It is not that the devoted student of Systema merely admires the founders; rather, he or she adores them. The founders are loved and treated as representatives of higher truths.

***

A common epithet used to dismiss Systema is 'cult.' And I can see why. After all, as this chapter has argued, Systema is not just a martial art but an explicit way of life akin to an ancient philosophical school. It has a particular way of viewing reality, a specific conception of the ideal human, and a guru speaking at the centre. Practitioners often wear similar clothes (camouflage pants and Systema-logo t-shirts) and undergo strange looking rites involving strikes and

---

[19] *Systema for Life Podcast*, Episode 13, featuring Ryo Onishi (December 30, 2017)
[20] *Systema for Life Podcast*, Episode 41, featuring Rob Poyton (July 20, 2018)

whips, all while training to alter their approach not only to combat but to daily existence.

It is not, however, for that reason a cult as the term is popularly understood. The word cult derives from the Latin word *cultus*, which itself derives from the verb *colere*, meaning variously "to cultivate, till, tend, take care of a field" and "to cherish, seek, practice, devote one's self to." *Cultus* translates to training and education, to care directed toward the refinement of life, as well as to veneration. Systema is a *cultus* in all these senses of the term.

When asked about the relationship between Russian Orthodox Christianity and his art, and whether non-believers could accept his teaching, Ryabko responds: "We are not a sect, nor are we imposing anything. They can take some ideas from the training and use them without necessarily converting to the religion."[21] In my experience, and in the experience of others around me, this seems true. No one in Systema attempts to cut others off from the world or to control their everyday behaviour through coercion or social pressure. The training is open to all and can end at any time. Nor is there any sort of tithing component to Systema, as there would be in a modern cult. Yes, of course, there are participation fees, but that is no different from a yoga or meditation class. We are not describing a tribute that one pays to the master. Classes are everyday economic transactions between consumers and a service provider.

Systema is a community made up of dedicated, sometimes overly-enthusiastic students who feel from their experiences with the art that it has something to show which other martial arts do not. They see in its training not only a cool set of learnable skills and a chance to blow off steam but also a viable way toward truth and happiness.

---

[21] https://web.archive.org/web/20160314103019/http://members.aikidojournal.com/private/interview-with-mikhail-ryabko/, accessed June 22, 2020

2. Traditions

Currently, when you click on the 'What is Systema?' tab on Headquarters' website you learn that the practice of Systema dates to the tenth century.[1] The art, the page goes on to say, emerged among proto-Russian knights facing an overwhelming number of opponents, forced to do battle on diverse terrain over many seasons. These knights were practical, deadly, and efficient, yet their art was easy to learn.

For centuries the knights taught their methods to other Russian warriors. But, after the revolution of 1917, the Bolsheviks suppressed the ancient ways. Common people throughout Russia could no longer practice as before. Instead, the tenth-century wisdom became one more tool of state oppression, wielded only by elite Russian military units.

Despite this period of misuse, Systema is non-destructive, serving only to build up and strengthen bodies and to cleanse minds of pride through the virtue of humility.

When the Systema-trained warrior is not engaged in self-defense or in the protection of others, "always causing the least possible damage" to opponents, he or she works to eliminate pride, aggression, greed, and envy from their heart.

Those who remain curious about Systema's origins are offered a list of books concerning Orthodox Christian spirituality, including a work written by the nineteenth-century monk Theophan the Recluse. There is also a link to a Russian website dedicated to a mode of prayer called Hesychasm (pronounced *hess-a-kism*). This generally involves breath-centred meditation and the evocation of the so-called Jesus Prayer, a fervent request for Christ to forgive one's sins. Its successful use is said to produce a feeling of stillness, or *heschyia*.

---

[1] https://www.russianmartialart.com/whatis.php, accessed September 26, 2016

All in all, this is an intriguing advertisement. Here the origin of Systema becomes the story of a lost secret, suppressed and misused by an evil government. This secret, now available for sale in the form of a civilian training regimen, promises to improve the functioning of bodies and the quality of souls. At the same time, it is a holy weapon to be used against evil forces.

***

Many historians make use of the category 'invented tradition.'[2] For the same reason, they also make use of the term 'myth.' As Roland Barthes explains, a myth is a speech act (oral, written, or iconographic) which possesses both a meaning and a form. The meaning of the myth is always derived from the contingencies of history; the form, however, presses aside that contingency to make room for more abstract ideas and concepts. It draws individuals to look into the past but then directs their gaze elsewhere, towards a value rather than towards a truth. In this way, Barthes asserts, myth "transforms history into nature."[3]

Invented traditions and myths are common. Wishing to legitimize innovations in practice or to retain a feeling of familiarity in a startling new world, groups engage with traditional stories, linking their present day experiences to those of an ancient, often medieval past, sometimes even seeking to revive a setting which never strictly speaking existed.[4]

---

[2] Eric Hobsbawn, "Introduction: Inventing Traditions," in *The Invention of Tradition*, edited by Eric Hobsbawn and T.O. Ranger (Cambridge University Press, 1983): 1-12; Richard Handler and Jocelyn Linnekin, "Tradition, Genuine or Spurious," *The Journal of American Folklore*, Volume 97, Number 385 (1984): 273
[3] Roland Barthes, *Mythologies*, translated by Richard Howard (Hill and Wang, 2013): 226-240
[4] See, for example, the commemorative use of medieval iconography and myth in the context of twentieth-century military culture in Stefan Goebel, *The Great War and Medieval Memory: War, Remembrance and Medievalism in Britain and Germany, 1914-1940* (Cambridge University Press, 2007)

Consider, for example, Kōdōkan Judo, developed by Kanō Jigorō in the late-nineteenth century. Studying wrestling, vital strike techniques, and the biodynamics of the human body, Jigorō produced a new form of Jiu Jitsu. It stressed competition and multiple attackers, eventually becoming the hand-to-hand combat method of the Tokyo police. He announced that his new school was "best suited to today's world," but selected the name Judo because it gave the art traditional resonance, allowing him to advertise it as a way or path toward character building and the efficient use of one's energy.[5] Jigorō invented something new from the received body of Jiu Jitsu and then linked a story about the ancient past to his modern product.

In this chapter, I would like to explore the possibility that Systema has done something similar.

***

When asked about their military records the founders of the art tend to demur, changing the subject. For example, when asked by Rob Poyton about his time training in the army or with Ryabko, Vasiliev characteristically responds: "This is a whole story in itself, perhaps we can address it sometime in the future."[6] And elsewhere, such as on the MoscowHQ webpage, we read statements like: "According to historical notes and sources, SYSTEMA remained in service of the

---

[5] Inoue Shun, "The Invention of the Martial Arts: Kanō Jigorō and Kōdōkan Judo," in *Mirror of Modernity: Invented Traditions in Modern Japan*, edited by Stephen Vlastos (University of California Press, 1998): 164-169

[6] *Systema Voices*, Volume One, edited by Rob Poyton (Cutting Edge, 2018): 31. Incidentally, this is a reprint of an interview from 2013 which has been slightly edited so that Poyton congratulates Vasiliev on the 25th anniversary of the opening of Systema Headquarters rather than on the 20th anniversary. See original here:
https://www.russianmartialart.com/article_info.php?articles_id=101
, accessed May 10, 2019

Soviet Army but all associated activities were classified as 'top secret.'"[7]

One result of this compartmentalization is something philosophers call an "epistemic absence," a place in the record where there is both a paucity of reliable information and substantial barriers to gaining such information. These epistemic absences, when they emerge, tend to be filled with tropes and familiar narratives rather than facts.[8]

The goal of this chapter is to attempt, using the methods of historiography, to fill the empty space created by "perhaps we can address it sometime in the future" and "Top Secret" with reasoned conjecture based on verifiable evidence, using reliable historical sources.

***

Systema's account of itself often alludes to war fighting and to Russian Special Purpose Units, also called Spetsnaz. Nevertheless, it insists on locating its origins in a distant past which is stereotypically Russian.[9] The MoscowHQ website notes that because the Slavic people were "behind other nations in weapons and professionalism, Slavs were superior in mastership, use of terrain conditions, organisation of reconnaissance, ambushes and sudden attacks or avoiding undesired battle – everything denoted by the term 'Scythian war.'"[10]

The word 'Scythian' would not be recognizable to your average Western reader, but those steeped in a particular historiographical tradition would know it immediately. The term, in a Russian context, probably refers to the sixth-century Zhazar "Turks" of southern Russia, a rebellious tribe

---

[7] http://systemaryabko.wixsite.com/systema/hostorical-roots, accessed May 13, 2019

[8] For more on the concept of epistemic absence, see Emma A. Jane and Chris Fleming, *Modern Conspiracy: The Importance of Being Paranoid* (Bloomsbury, 2014): Ch. 3

[9] Spetsnaz is a shortened version of *Voyska Spetsialnovo Naznacheniya* or Special Purpose Units.

[10] http://systemaryabko.wixsite.com/systema/hostorical-roots, accessed May 13, 2019

of warriors from Mongolia who broke free from their overlords and created their own nation.[11] They were supposedly renowned for their ability to battle on horseback, striking quickly and retreating, wearing down their larger, more powerful adversaries. Some modern Eurasianists, Russian nationalists who embrace an imperialist view of the state, conceive of themselves as descendants or reincarnations of the ancient Scythians.[12]

Knowing this helps to makes sense of MoscowHQ's clarification that

> "the notion 'Russian' means martial art that had been born long before the time when Kievan Russia joined Eastern Slavs, current Russians, Ukrainians and Byelorussians into unified Russian nation. Being born as a means for necessary self-defense of freedom-loving nation, the art of hand-to-hand combat was perfected in military princely bands of men and hardened in the Battle of the Ice and the Battle of Kulikovo."

The Battle of the Ice is the name of the conflict in which the legendary hero Alexander Nevsky is said to have led an army of 2500 soldiers against a force twice that size maintained by the Republic of Novgorod. That battle occurred in 1242. The Battle of Kulikovo, which occurred in 1380, names a contest between the forces of the Prince of Moscow and the larger armies of the Golden Horde.

What is fascinating about the MoscowHQ account is not how little it tells us about the origins of Systema and how much instead it works to identify the art not just with Russia but with Russian-ness itself.

Take the reference to Nevsky. This is, in the popular and official imagination of Russia today, a reference to the

---

[11] Margaret Meserve, *Empires of Islam in Renaissance Historical Thought* (Harvard University Press, 2008): 18-20

[12] Charles Clover, *Black Wind, White Snow: The Rise of Russia's New Nationalism* (Yale University Press, 2016): 53

nation's greatest war leader and statesman. Nevsky represents, according to historian Gregory Carleton, the Russian people's self-conception as a beleaguered nation, which—despite its disadvantages—succeeds in defending its freedom against all odds. Furthermore, he represents the historical moment in which Russians embraced and maintained their identification with Orthodox Christianity. Without Nevsky, Russia would have fallen, materially and spiritually.[13]

The reference to the Battle of Kulikovo is equally as revealing. In 2003 the Russian Federation's Ministry of Defense published a three volume military history of their nation. This recounting of all of Russia's many wars depicts the Battle of Kulikovo as a moment of Russian sacrifice in which Europe was shielded from the hordes of Genghis Khan. Kulikovo, in this sense, represents the Russian people's conception of themselves as martyrs, as those who lay down their lives for a greater good. It also evokes, indirectly, the concept of the Russian motherland itself, associated as it is with the image of the Virgin Mary, the mother of Christ. Dmitry Donskoy, now a canonized Russian Orthodox saint, prior to entering into the battle of Kulikovo, is said to have summoned his forces while in Mary's church and to have prayed afterwards in her name.[14]

Systema Headquarters' page evokes these same ideas. Alluding to *John 15:13*, the page reads:

> "The Word of God in the bible tells us that there is no bigger sacrifice than to give up your life for others. Thus, anyone who prepares to be a true warrior, who undergoes training and takes a weapon in his hand, accepts this possibility of sacrificing his life in the name of love for

---

[13] It should be noted that Nevsky is also treated as the patron saint of Russia's Federal Security Service, the agency which replaced the Soviet KGB. See Gregory Carleton, *Russia: The Story of War* (Harvard Belknap Press, 2017): 211-213
[14] *Ibid*: 24-29

other people; in essence, he prepares to become a martyr."[15]

From all of this then, we can see that Systema, places its beginning not just in an ancient past but in an ancient past which is understood to reflect something quintessential about Russia as a nation: self-sacrificing, pious, and courageous.

An intensely nationalist version of history has been inserted into the epistemic absence produced by "perhaps we can address it sometime in the future" and "Top Secret." This version says, it seems to me, that Systema is in essence not just a martial art *from* Russia but that it *is* Russia.

***

How might we put Systema's account of itself into a modern historiographical context? What story would emerge then?

When Systema Headquarters' webpage makes reference to tenth-century knights and MoscowHQ speaks of "military princely bands of men," the authors are likely alluding to the *Malaia Druzhinas*, bands of twenty five to several hundred who served as personal protection or law enforcement for feudal princes.[16] The *Malaia Druzhinas* fought on horseback, using a broadsword and shield. Their close quarter skills likely included basic wrestling techniques, the use of the dagger, long and short lances, two-handed and single-handed swords, and the handling of pole arms.[17]

It seems to me then that Systema, assuming that it indeed found its roots in the early medieval era and was indeed a direct descendent of the *Malaia Druzhinas*, would today teach horse riding, swordplay, and archery, and would accustom its practitioners to the weight of chain mail.

---

[15] https://russianmartialart.com/whatis.php, accessed May 20, 2019
[16] David Nicolle and Angus McBride, *Armies of Medieval Russia, 750-1250* (Osprey Publishing Limited, 1999): 18-19
[17] Sydney Angelo, *The Martial Arts of Renaissance Europe* (Yale University Press, 2000): 26

Admittedly, we *can* point to at least one potential example of medieval practice in modern Systema. There is the record of Ryabko's use of the *shashka*, a Russian sabre. As early as 2003, Ryabko is documented having taught seminars with the use of this sword.[18] We also see sword work in YouTube videos from 2013 and 2015.[19] However, a quick Wikipedia search reveals that this sabre was adopted by the Russian military in the late nineteenth century so we need not assume a medieval origin.

In contrast to the *Malaia Druzhinas*, examine the *Lochama Ba'Terror* course instituted by the Israeli military in the 1960s.[20] The course lasts one-and-a-half months and involves training in hand-to-hand combat and knife work. Participants learn to take strikes to the stomach and face using breathing to maintain emotional stability. The goal is to teach soldiers how to access their violent instincts and to instill the capacity for determined action. They learn how to be beaten so that they can then attack without fear.[21]

Although Systema does not seek to foster aggressive responses to violence as Israeli martial artists do, the two methods are nonetheless very similar. Both seek to level out the distinctions between criminal and military violence, and to prepare bodies and minds for sudden shifts in intensity. And they both do this through heavy body contact and emotion work.[22] In Russia, it appears that such training

---

[18] https://web.archive.org/web/20160314103019/http://members.aikidojournal.com/private/interview-with-mikhail-ryabko/, accessed June 22, 2020

[19] https://www.youtube.com/watch?v=oFMuBts3jng and https://www.youtube.com/watch?v=0q0dCtSQG5Y, accessed May 22, 2019

[20] Einat Bar-On Cohen, "Globalization of the War on Violence: Israeli Close-Combat Krav Maga and Sudden Alterations in Intensity," *Social Anthropology*, Volume 18, Number 3 (2010): 272

[21] Limor Samimian-Darash, "Rebuilding the Body Through Violence and Control," *Ethnography*, Volume 14, Number 1 (2012): 52-58

[22] Einat Bar-On Cohen, "Globalization of the War on Violence": 272-275, 282

began in the 1920s from a mixture of traditional wrestling, Judo and Jiu Jitsu, and was later adopted by Spetsnaz.[23]

What all of this suggests to me is that, despite the tradition which Systema Headquarters and MoscowHQ attach to their art, there is little reason to assent to the claim that Systema is, in its entirety, a product of the medieval era which has survived into the present day. Not only does it look very little like any known ancient martial art in either the West or the East, but it very strongly resembles other well-documented modern counter-terror training methods.

It seems to me rather that the things out of which Systema was built are all modern in origin. These things—nineteenth- and twentieth-century European physical culture, twentieth-century Russian militarism, and the post-nineteenth-century Russian embrace of Orthodox monasticism—are, we might say, the building blocks of the 'System.'

***

All of that said, we can easily imagine that some aspect of what is today called Systema may indeed have been co-opted by the Soviets for military use. The historical record shows that Communist states, at least in a constrained way, took up breathing arts and calisthenics as part of their characteristically large-scale moral reform efforts.

Communist China, for instance, developed such arts. Qigong, which means breath training, was created by Huang Yueting in 1949 from traditional body techniques and modern physiological knowledge. It was meant to be used, and for two or three years was used, to heal Chinese bodies and to strengthen the state generally, particularly against the dangers of neurasthenia, a disorder of the nerves associated with the unique pressures of modern living.[24]

Meanwhile, Stalinist Russia, in an effort to promote child birth, banned abortion and extolled the necessity of

---

[23] Mark Galeotti, *Spetsnaz: Russia's Special Forces* (Osprey Publishing Ltd., 2015): 61
[24] David A. Palmer, *Qigong Fever: Body, Science, and Utopia in China* (Columbia University Press, 2007): 29-30

producing strong children. Unfortunately, however, the state did not have enough pain-relieving nitrous oxide to perform the extra number of births. In response, psychologist I.Z. Vel'vovskii, after having studied hypnosis in the 1920s and 1930s, developed a method of pain relief called psychoprophylaxis, an early precursor of Lamaze training.

In Vel'vovskii's own words, psychoprophylaxis was a "system of measures aimed at preventing the appearance and development of labor pain effected through influences exerted on the higher dimensions of the central nervous system."[25] This system involved sexual education, patterned breathing, light massage, and teaching how to bear down properly. Vel'vovskii believed that it was culture and conditioning that had instilled in women a fear of childbirth; this fear was the source of their pain. In order to eliminate such pain, bodies needed to be reconditioned.[26] The Soviet state, looking for an inexpensive, easy-to-use solution to its lack of nitrous oxide, tried to make psychoprophylaxis a common method of pain-relief.

We can see from the examples of Qigong and psychoprophylaxis that communist states were willing to incorporate body techniques such as breathing, massage, and meditation into their biopolitical regimes, all for the purpose of increasing the overall strength and size of their polities. Indeed, this enthusiasm for eugenics was not uncommon in the early twentieth century world.

Western intellectuals had been thinking about the relationship between body and state at least since the days of Plato, but not with the intensity and fervor that we find in the nineteenth and early-twentieth centuries. Europeans, and then the rest of the world, responded to the Industrial Revolution and the first truly globalized economy with

---

[25] Paula A. Michaels, *Lamaze: An International History* (Oxford University Press, 2014): 33
[26] *Ibid*: 35-37

trepidation. Modernity, they worried, was causing mankind to degenerate.[27]

Scandinavian Gymnasts, such as Pehr Henrik Ling, had in the previous generation developed complex 'movement cures' involving exercises and posture practices designed to restore health and spiritual well-being to his patients. Eugene Sandow, the Arnold Schwarzenegger of the nineteenth century, then began to popularize such techniques in his magazines and instructions books. He viewed the body as sacred, its movements and health manifestations of one's degree of inner well-being.[28] He, and many members of his audience, marked the body as a site of spiritual concern and moral development.

Some Hindu Indians, colonized by the British Empire, took up these ideas. They, like their European counterparts, also expressed an enthusiasm for eugenic thought. They began to view their subjugation as a form of spiritual and physical degeneration. Nationalist yogis like Swami Kuvalayanada published how-to manuals in the art of posture practice, announcing—in words that explicitly echoed the writings of men like Sandow—the physical, mental, and spiritual benefits of yoga. Meditation, breathing, and posture practice were taken to be a means of directly improving not only one's physical health but the genetic quality of mankind as a whole.[29]

Late nineteenth-century British and American practitioners of physical culture who read translations of these Indian how-to manuals believed them to be a fount of ancient wisdom. In fact, however, they were only reading back to themselves the fruits of their own beliefs and practices.

---

[27] On this topic generally, see Daniel Pick, *Faces of Degeneration: A European Disorder, c. 1848-1918* (Cambridge University Press, 1989) and Marius Turda, *Modernity and Eugenics* (Palgrave University Press, 2010)
[28] Mark Singleton, *Yoga Body: The Origins of Modern Posture Practice* (Oxford University Press, 2010): 84-90
[29] *Ibid*: 115-120

Blending *asana* with Protestant Christian spirituality, women such as Genevieve Stebbins began to popularize yogic posture practice through their own manuals and specialty fitness magazines. Her *Dynamic Breathing and Harmonic Gymnastics: A Complete System of Psychical, Aesthetic and Physical Culture* (1892) offered a regimen of callisthenic movement, deep breathing, relaxation, and visualization exercises designed to balance mind and body for the purposes of achieving a state of spiritual enlightenment, a feminine form of so-called 'muscular Christianity.'[30]

While in Germany, early Bauhaus students, adhering to the recently-founded philosophy Mazdaznan, practiced similar physical exercises, albeit with the intention of improving awareness and creativity. Through elaborate dance routines, they sought to absorb into themselves God's life-breath, strengthening their nervous systems and raising themselves above the so-called lesser races.[31]

A new industry emerged in the early twentieth century among European nations as a response to these ideas. At the centre of this new industry was the concept of 'will.' The aim was to teach individuals, faced with the pressures of mass society and fast-paced life, to gain control over their runaway desires. Modernity itself, some held, was the cause of "nervousness" or neurasthenia, a state of being in which society ruled over bodies and minds rather than vice versa.[32]

One cure frequently offered for this most modern of conditions, the condition of a weak or disordered will, was bodily exercise. In Germany, body culture magazines such as *Strength and Beauty* (1901) and *The Man of Culture: Magazine for Self-Discipline of Body and Mind* (1904) offered exercises designed to improve physical fitness and nervous

---

[30] *Ibid*: 144-147
[31] Linn Burchert, "The Spiritual Enhancement of the Body: Johannes Itten, Gertrud Grunow, and Mazdaznan at the Early Bauhaus," in *Bauhaus Bodies: Gender, Sexuality, and Body Culture in Modernism's Legendary Art School*, edited by Elizabeth Otto and Patrick Rössler (Bloomsbury, 2019): 51, 61
[32] Michael Cowen, *Cult of the Will: Nervousness and German Modernity* (Penn State University Press, 2008): 8-9

hygiene.[33] Dutchman Jorgen Peter Muller's *My System*, selling over one million copies in Germany alone, provided similar guidance. His books prized efficient action, and instructed readers in exercises meant to instill beautiful strength and thus a pure, unsullied will.[34]

Russians, like most other industrializing, globalizing peoples, embraced the physical culture of the nineteenth- and twentieth-century German states. Pyotr Lesgaft, the namesake of the Lesgaft National State University of Physical Education, Sport, and Health in St. Petersburg, absorbed many of the ideas associated with the movement cure and with other aspects of European physical culture, including concerns over the will and eugenics. At the end of the nineteenth-century, Lesgaft was tapped to advise the Russian military on the best methods of training cadets.[35] Through him, European physical culture become an institutionalized part of Russian military culture.

At the same time, Russia also had its own famous, magazine-publishing, Sandow-like bodybuilder named Ivan Lebedev. He represented to Russians the image of the strongman peasant, the ideal Russia worker.[36] During the Soviet era, men like Lenin and Stalin looked to the practices of men like Lebedev for tools to forge the New Soviet Man. Lenin encouraged the practice of exercise and hygiene for the sake of the Revolution.[37] And after the Revolution had succeeded, in the 1920s, the state, in propaganda if not in reality, encouraged Russians to take bodily care of themselves

---

[33] *Ibid*: 112-113
[34] *Ibid*: 123-130; Singleton, *Yoga Body*: 98. Precursors of these ideas date back as early as 1793. See Felix Saure, "Beautiful Bodies, Exercising Warriors and Original Peoples: Sports, Greek Antiquity and National Identity from Winckelmann to 'Turnvater Jahn'," *German History*, Volume 27, Number 3 (2009): 365-370
[35] Susan Grant, *Physical Culture and Sport in Soviet Society: Propaganda, Acculturation, and Transformation in the 1920s and 1930s* (Routledge, 2012): 11-24
[36] *Ibid*: 10-13
[37] Susan Grant, "Bolsheviks, Revolution, and Physical Culture," *The International Journal of the History of Sport*, Volume 31, Number 7 (2014): 726-729

through the practice of physical culture.[38] Many Russians, soldiers and civilians alike, took up breathing, exercise, and posture practice in order to strengthen the nation and to ward off the degenerative effects of modern living.

***

Physical culture, the cult of the will, and eugenics are, in a sense, secular responses to anxieties inspired by the modern world. Systema, although it shares in these secular concerns and responds to them through the same measures—through breathing, exercise, and posture practice—participates also in what we might call a spiritual response to modernity.

Hesychasm, as mentioned before, is a mode of prayer associated with Orthodox Christianity. While Catholicism, centred at Rome, looked to the writings of the Latin Church Fathers, Orthodox Christians looked to the Desert and Cappadocian Fathers such as Evagrios Ponticos and Gregory of Nyssa. These Greek-speaking Fathers, closely associated with the monks of the Egyptian desert, wrote numerous guides to Christian prayer and correct living.

Evagrios, for instance, writing in the fourth century, in his numerous guides to monastic practice, instructed Christians to seek out stillness or *heschyia* above all else. The Christian "must be like a soldier of Christ, detached from material things, free from cares and not involved in trade or commerce." Through a combination of bodily deprivations such as fasting and sleepless vigils, visualization exercises regarding death and Judgement, and a prayer detached from the imagination, Evagrios claimed that one could overcome the influence of demons and the desire for glory. In this state of prayer, the monk came to resemble an angel.[39] This

---

[38] Susan Grant, "The *Fizkul'tura* Generation: Modernizing Lifestyles in Early Soviet Russia," *The Soviet and Post-Soviet Review*, Volume 37, (2010): 147-151, 160-161

[39] Evagrios Ponticos, "Outline Teaching on Asceticism and Stillness in the Solitary Life," "Texts on Discrimination in Respect of Passions and Thoughts," and "On Prayer," in *Philokalia*, Volume One, edited and translated by G.E.H Palmer, Philip Sharrard, and Kallistos Ware (Farrar, Straus and Giroux, 1983): 31, 36-39, 67-68

angelic state would eventually become associated with the quality of stillness.

For example, the seventh-century Christian monk John Climacus, well-familiar with Evagrian desert spirituality, later wrote in his *Ladder of Divine Ascent* that "stillness of the body is the accurate knowledge and management of one's feelings and perceptions. Stillness of soul is the accurate knowledge of one's thoughts and is an unassailable mind."[40] Here Climacus explicitly echoes Evagrios, writing later that "a hesychast is like an angel on earth."[41]

Over the next two centuries, as techniques for producing stillness continued to develop, authors such as Hesychios the Priest incorporated new breath-centred meditations into their prayer regimen.

In *On Watchfulness and Holiness*, Hesychios cites four methods of attaining holiness: humility, fasting, prayer, and watchfulness. To be watchful involved scrutinizing one's mental images, scanning them at all times for demonic influence. When demonic influence had been detected, one repeatedly called on Christ's mercy and remembered the lone fact of death in order to clear the mind of images.[42] In doing so, one could let breathing lead one's prayer. "With your breathing combine watchfulness and the name of Jesus, or humility and the unremitting study of death. Both may confer great blessing." Those sufficiently blessed through assiduous practice became like a spider, still at the centre of its web, alert to all sinful thoughts, awake to all spiritual dangers.[43]

This breath-centred element of prayer, being the dominant mode of monastic practice institutionalized at Mt. Athos in the fourteenth century, would become a cornerstone of

---

[40] John Climacus, *The Ladder of Divine Ascent*, translated by Colm Luidheid and Norman Russell (Paulist Press, 1982): 262
[41] *Ibid*: 263
[42] Hesychos the Priest, "On Watchfulness and Holiness," in *Philokalia*, Volume One, edited and translated by G.E.H Palmer, Philip Sharrard, and Kallistos Ware (Farrar, Straus and Giroux, 1983): 164-165
[43] *Ibid*: 166

Orthodox spirituality. The version of the Jesus Prayer practiced by Gregory Palamas and Nikephoros the Monk involved sitting on a low stool, chin to chest, after the example of Elijah in *1 Kings 18:42*. In this position, requesting Christ's intervention, one imagined their breath entering through the nostrils, down into the lungs and into the heart, bringing with it the feeling of the intellect descending into the centre of one's being, to where God's light illuminates directly.[44]

That said, Hesychasm did not become part of mainstream Russian Orthodox life until the nineteenth century, with the publishing of *The Way of the Pilgrim* and the translation efforts of Theophan the Recluse. First published in 1881, the *Way of the Pilgrim* was a popular guide to prayer. It told the story of a young man's quest to learn how to pray and to live the correct way of life. The unnamed pilgrim is led to embrace the Christian luminaries collected in the *Philokalia*, a multi-volume collection containing the writings of Evagrios, Hesychios, Gregory Palamas, Nikephoros, and many other Greek Fathers. The pilgrim learns of breath-centred prayer and how to pray unceasingly, calling on Christ to forgive his sins thousands of times per day.[45]

The publishing of the *Way of the Pilgrim* coincided with Theophan the Recluse's translation of the *Philokalia* from Greek into Russian, released in five volumes in 1886.[46] Suddenly, Russians of the late nineteenth-century had popular and scholarly access to hesychast practice and theology.

***

---

[44] Kallistos Ware, "'My Helper and My Enemy': The Body in Greek Christianity," in *Religion and the Body*, edited by Sarah Coakley (Cambridge University Press, 1997): 106-107; Dirk Krausmüller, "The Rise of Hesychasm," in *The Cambridge History of Christianity: Eastern Christianity*, edited by Michael Angold (Cambridge University Press, 2008): 103-104
[45] Anonymous, *The Way of the Pilgrim*, translated by Gleb Pokrovsky (Skylight Paths Publishing, 2001): 17, 21
[46] Vassa Kontoma, "The Philokalia," in *The Orthodox Christian World*, edited by Augustine Casidy (Routledge, 2012): 460-461

Russia has always been strongly associated with the Orthodox faith, even if under Communism this association was weakened. True, the early Bolsheviks had by 1937 largely eliminated churches and monasteries in Russia but this did not last. Stalin, in order to bolster support for the Second World War, was forced to reinstate the Patriciate in 1943. And while, yes, the church was heavily policed and tightly controlled under Communism, there were still over thirty million Orthodox believers in the nation and over 5000 churches.[47] Since the fall of Communism, that number has risen to over 20,000, with roughly 700 monasteries.[48] Today's Russians, like their counterparts in the West, may not attend church regularly. Nonetheless, the majority strongly identify themselves as Orthodox Christian.[49] Indeed, since 1995, there has been an explosion in the media use of the term 'traditional religion' with respect to Orthodoxy, and more recently a spike in the use of the term 'spiritual security'.[50] Many Russians, post-Communism, have returned to viewing themselves as a militantly Orthodox nation.

This connection is especially strong in the security services. Under Communism, the life of a solider was never glamorous. It was often downright terrorizing. New recruits arrived every six months and served for two years. The pay was low, living conditions poor, training rudimentary, and hazing rife. New recruits would enter into a world of physical abuse, theft, extortion, and forced labour as older, more experienced soldiers, the *stariki* or grandfathers, took advantage of the fresh meat. If that were not enough, the Soviet leadership often lied to their soldiers about the nature of their missions and threw them into the field unprepared.[51]

---

[47] Nickolas Lupinin, "The Russian Orthodox Church," in *Eastern Christianity and the Cold War, 1945-1991* (Routledge, 2010): 20-35
[48] Shevzov, "The Russian Tradition" in *The Orthodox Christian World*: 33
[49] Geraldine Fagan, *Believing in Russia: Religious Policy After Communism* (Routledge, 2013): 24-26
[50] *Ibid*: 95-121
[51] Roger R. Reese, *The Soviet Military Experience: A History of the Soviet Army, 1917-1991* (Routledge, 2000): 167-170

When the Soviet Union began the process of dissolution in 1989, injury was added to abuse. Outgoing Soviets slashed the military's budget by 14.2% and reduced its size by 12%.[52] Many soldiers received their pink slips, so to speak. As a consequence, in the mid-90s, the Orthodox Church, partly as an act of charity and partly out of political acumen, forged a renewed alliance with the Russian military, as well as with the border guards and the Ministry of Interior Affairs. The Church began to provide money, support, and education to downcast Russian soldiers.[53] Religion, including popular Hesychast theology, came rushing back to fill the void left by political reform.

***

What we have then in Systema is a martial art that 1) resembles modern counter-terror training methods in every respect and lacks any obvious connection to the tactics and weaponry of the medieval era; that 2) labels itself explicitly as a system of physical culture, openly espousing concerns for the national body and incorporating elements of Christian doctrine, all within the context of breathwork and posture practice; and that 3) expresses a form of popular Hesychasm in which practitioners seek to attain an attitude of stillness through the use of breath-centered prayer.

All three of the above characteristics—the military training, the physical culture directed against the deleterious effects of modernity, the close association with monastic strands of Orthodox Christianity—are easily located in the Spetsnaz units of the Ministry of Interior Affairs, where—as we shall see—Ryabko served for many years.

If Systema is a martial art born of medieval Russia, then it is also a way of life born in response to the institutions and conditions of the modern Russian world.

---

[52] *Ibid*: 174-175
[53] John Gerrard and Carol Gerrard, *Russian Orthodoxy Resurgent: Faith and Power in the New Russia* (Princeton University Press, 2008): 219-223

3. Foundations

In the previous chapter, I attempted to reframe the given history of Systema, placing the art into a larger, modern historical context. Here I would like, to the extent that it's possible, to focus in on the lives of Ryabko and Vasiliev themselves. It seems to me that looking closely at the founders of Systema will further highlight the modern rather than medieval nature of the Russian Martial Art.

The account which emerges from a cross-referencing of stories told in various published interviews and off-hand comments is one of development over time.

It is an account of two Soviet soldiers who, having been deployed elsewhere for a short period, in the early 80s found themselves working together in the city of Tver, instructing a police division of a Russian security service. Meeting under these conditions, they struck up a friendship. For a brief while, Ryabko taught Vasiliev a new way of approaching martial arts, one directed more towards peace rather than destruction. However, shortly before the collapse of the Soviet Union, Vasiliev left Russia and travelled to North America. Ryabko continued along with his military career and martial arts practice, while Vasiliev sought to make a living in a new country. Eventually, due to his martial ability and the mystique of foreign expertise, Vasiliev opened a successful martial arts club in Toronto.

Despite this distance, the two men kept in touch as best they could. Ryabko taught in his inimitable way with his own students while Vasiliev did likewise with his, even as he attempted to emulate his master. Finally, in the beginning of the new millennium, the two men reunited. This is when Systema in Toronto began to shift from a primarily combative art to one more explicitly devoted to crafting a way of living centred on breathing and relaxation exercises. This was also when Systema entered a global marketplace, fully embracing product branding and other marketing tools, including the heavy use of social media.

***

Mikhail Ryabko was born in Belorussia on May 6th, 1961.[1] This much appears certain. Otherwise I'm not sure what to think. Ryabko himself states that he began studying martial arts as a youth under the tutelage of his father and grandfather.[2] This seems to me reasonable to accept. Past that, things become a matter of interpretation.

Scott Meredith, in *Let Every Breath...,* reports that Ryabko was conscripted into the special purpose units of Russia at age fifteen.[3] This, if true, would place him in a Spetsnaz unit in 1976. However, dates given on Ryabko's previous website contradict this. An 'about' page on the old MoscowHQ website, now removed from the internet but captured by the Internet Archive, states that Ryabko entered Agricultural and Technical school in 1976 and that he did not join the Russian military until 1981, when he would have been 20. The website had also stated that his time with the Ministry of

---

[1] Google search result: https://g.co/kgs/C6G9um, accessed May 10, 2019
[2] https://web.archive.org/web/20160314103019/http://members.aikidojournal.com/private/interview-with-mikhail-ryabko/, accessed June 22, 2020
[3] Vladimir Vasiliev and Scott Meredith, *Let Every Breath...: Secrets of the Russian Breath Masters* (Russian Martial Art, 2006): 35

Interior Affairs (MVD) did not begin until 1983, when he would have been 22.[4]

Basing my judgement on the information given on Ryabko's own official website, it seems more reasonable to suppose that, while Ryabko privately studied martial arts his entire life, his involvement with the Russian military and Spetsnaz probably did not begin until young adulthood.

Other things reported about Ryabko are similarly difficult to interpret. For instance, Ryabko claims in an interview conducted in 2013 to have been involved in operations against "armed groups, militias, terrorism, counterfeit currency, and hostage situations," including a hostage situation involving a school and pregnant women.[5] This statement very likely refers to the Beslan school siege which occurred in September 2004. Beslan seems to feature prominently in Systema's view of human evil. The Systema HQ website, to cite it once again, tells us that "training to be a true warrior is not only justified, but is necessary. How else can we save innocent people from evil? We all have seen the events of Beslan."[6] But, if Ryabko's remarks are meant to

---

[4] "Mikhail Vasilevich Ryabko one of the founders and developer of Russian warrior traditions and also the main instructor of Systema - the martial art of ancient Russia. Born 6th May, 1961 in Belorussia.
- In 1976 after completing form 8 he entered Agricultural and Technical School.
- From 1981 to 1983: Military service for USSR.
- From 1983 to 1993: he worked in the Security service of the Ministry of Interior Affairs of USSR, training security personnel from the Ministry.
- From 1989 to 1994: he started at the institute of Justice at the Ministry of Interior Affairs.
For ten years he served in special teams; participated in military operations, hostage release and he was an instructor at the centre of rapid response special teams." For a surprisingly thoughtful analysis of Ryabko's potential lineage which incorporates this material, see:
https://www.bullshido.net/forums/showthread.php?t=64255, accessed May 16, 2019
[5] https://da2el.wordpress.com/2013/05/29/interview-with-mikhail-ryabko-re-relaxing, accessed May 16, 2019
[6] https://russianmartialart.com/whatis.php, accessed May 13, 2019

refer to Beslan, then this does not seem to track with other available accounts. Not only does the Systema HQ website state between 2000-2002 that Ryabko was "the Chief Instructor of tactical training for the Emergency Response Team of MVD,"[7] but, in an interview conducted in 2003, Ryabko also states that he had by that time retired, serving only as a consultant.[8] It does not seem to me then that Ryabko, working as either an instructor or consultant, would have been *directly* involved in operations such as Beslan, assuming my inference is correct.

Here perhaps I should simply employ the principle of parsimony, giving the founder of Systema the benefit of the doubt. The simplest explanation is likely the correct one. By 2003, Ryabko had retired from active duty (perhaps even from his duties as an MVD tactical instructor) so that he could take up a different, higher bureaucratic position. It was perhaps from *that* position, outside the Ministry of Interior Affairs, away from the circle of direct action, that he was involved in operations. After all, Ryabko appears to have built for himself, post-Spetsnaz, a lengthy career in civil administration, having previously served as a Counsellor in Justice with the Ministry of Justice.[9]

Whatever the truth of Ryabko's service and whatever the weaknesses of my reasoned speculation, what I take from all of this—Ryabko's work for the MVD, his association with the

---

[7] https://web.archive.org/web/20010404213816/http://www.russian martialart.com:80/about/bios.html, accessed June 22, 2020
[8] https://web.archive.org/web/20160314103019/http://members.aiki dojournal.com/private/interview-with-mikhail-ryabko/, accessed June 22, 2020
[9] http://systemaryabko.wixsite.com/systema/the-founder, accessed May 13, 2019. According their website, "The Ministry of Justice (*Minyust*) is a federal executive body responsible for drafting and implementing government policy and legal regulation in …the penal system, registration of non-profit organisations… the bar and notary system, state registration of vital statistics, compliance of courts with the established operating procedure and implementation of court decisions and enactments by other agencies…" For the full description, see http://government.ru/en/department/99/events/, accessed August 28, 2019

Ministry of Justice, his references to domestic terrorism and criminality—is that we ought to think of Systema as something primarily born out of an involvement with law enforcement rather than war fighting. If I am correct, then we ought to think of Ryabko as a militarized SWAT team captain and course instructor who later went on to become an administrative authority in, say, the Federal Bureau of Prisons. Yes, we have good reason to suspect, based on his comments, that he was deployed for a time out of country, perhaps even in Afghanistan. I am not denying any wartime experiences. What I am saying is that, at least according to the information previously given on his official website, much of Ryabko's military career appears to have been spent as part of the domestic security service.[10]

The above analogy might not sit well with some. This is primarily because most people don't have a proper grasp of what Spetsnaz were under the Soviets.

For many the word evokes a story propagated in the West during the Cold War, primarily through the works of a Russian defector named Vladimir Bogdanovich Rezun, who took the pen name of Viktor Suvorov. Rezun portrayed Spetsnaz units as invincible shadow warriors, men who never held defensive positions, struck suddenly in the night before disappearing, and trained in only the most lethal and brutal environments. These were the soldiers prepared to go behind enemy lines and disable American or European nuclear

---

[10] "There are many sad things in war. I try to forget those things. Of course, I don't like war…"
https://da2el.wordpress.com/2013/05/29/interview-with-mikhail-ryabko-re-relaxing, accessed May 17, 2019.

capabilities.[11] Journalists were only too happy to accept this mythology.[12]

Today, having had access to Soviet archives for many years, researchers know better. When they speak of Spetsnaz, they are mostly speaking about young men (aged 18-20) with two years of training, guided by one or two experienced officers, who tended to perform recon missions in support of the Navy or Army.[13] These soldiers, albeit better trained than regular soldiers, in no way resembled the special forces of the West, either in capability or purpose.

---

[11] Viktor Suvorov, *Spetsnaz: The Story Behind the Soviet SAS*, translated by David Floyd (Hamish Hamilton, 1987): 2, 115-117

[12] A quote included in a newspaper feature story on Vasiliev in 2002 gives us a flavor of what people think of when they think about Spetsnaz: "But the Spetsnaz training was beyond rigorous. His instructors beat him every day and gave him electric shocks to toughen him. He had his arms bent behind him 'until you started screaming because you couldn't take the pain any more,' and then he would be jabbed with a knife. 'They wanted to see to what extreme you could go before breaking. They also used this exercise to teach you how to relax under pain and open up new personal potentials for endurance.' There were cold-weather swims — there's an SOU saying that 'the water is too cold for swimming only if it's ice' — and he was forced to fall on to huge anthills and let thousands of insects bite him. He was taken to morgues and serious car crashes and forced to carry dead bodies to make him less sensitive to the 'gore and pain.' The aim, he says, was to create a soldier 'immune to the psychological torment of battle. They wanted their elite special operations units not to fear death.'"
https://web.archive.org/web/20020603130403/http://russianmartial art.org/fightman.html, accessed Jan 1, 2017.
It is certainly worth noting that the above story does not appear to be the result of an interview *per se*. The account is taken almost verbatim from Vladimir Vasiliev, *The Russian System Guidebook* (Kindle Edition), Chapter Two, "Soviet Special Units Trainings," Location 100

[13] Robert D. Smith, "Western Misconceptions," in *Inside Spetsnaz-Soviet Special Operations: A Critical Analysis*, edited by Major William H. Burgess III (Presido, 1990): 21-24

Spetsnaz, they've determined, served to fill gaps in the lumbering Soviet military.[14] Throughout their existence, and especially in the 80s, they were used as light infantry, rapid-response strike forces, ambush units, and for intelligence gathering. Yet even as ambush units they had to rely on the support of airstrikes and heavy artillery to eliminate targets.[15] After Russia's withdrawal from Afghanistan, during the collapse of Communism, these same units were repurposed as body guards and internal security troops.[16] This last image, Spetsnaz as militarized police officers, probably best represents the nature of Ryabko's training in the mid-to-late 80s, especially given his connection to the Ministry of Interior Affairs, a Ministry which at the same time maintained its own domestically-purposed Spetsnaz units.

But, having located Ryabko for the most part in a realm of domestic law enforcement rather than international conflict, we are still left with the puzzle of Systema itself. When and for what reason, under what conditions, did Ryabko develop his System? After all, the footage of Ryabko demonstrating knife disarmament recorded in 1988 does not resemble his work of today, or even much the work shown in the early 2000s.[17] The martial art demonstrated by Ryabko in 1988 resembles rather, to my novice eye, the variation on Jiu-Jitsu that we would expect to see in Spetsnaz, at least according to the research of the previous chapter. When did that martial artist, the Ryabko of 1988, develop into the Ryabko of today?

---

[14] Mark Galeotti, *Spetsnaz: Russia's Special Forces* (Osprey Publishing Ltd., 2015): 5-6, 20-23
[15] Tony Balasevicous, *Squandering the Capability: Soviet SOF in Afghanistan* (Canadian Defense Academy Press, 2011): 15-17
[16] Galeotti, *Spetsnaz*: 28
[17] Compare the footage of 1988 recorded in Russia (https://www.youtube.com/watch?v=eRDMmbTFX90, accessed May 13, 2019) with that recorded at Systema Headquarters in 2000 (https://www.youtube.com/watch?v=5F_qGqPFbF4, accessed May 15, 2019) and with that recorded in 2015 (https://www.youtube.com/watch?v=nG43FXkO_x4, accessed May 15, 2019)

We cannot answer this question directly, but perhaps we can infer something from the available facts.

***

Vladimir Vasiliev, to my knowledge, has never published his date of birth. Nonetheless, a little digging reveals that he was born on December 3rd, very probably in 1960.[18] He grew up in Tver and was conscripted into the Russian military in 1977, undergoing "specialized military training" at age 18.[19] During this time he also studied boxing and hand-to-hand combat. Having completed in 1979 his mandatory service with the Russian military, he transferred into "a different service," and took up the practice of Karate, becoming at some point "fourth in all of Russia."[20]

Only a handful of facts can help us to piece together a rough timeline of what came next. Vasiliev reports that he was "over twenty years old" when he began his career as a Spetsnaz instructor, teaching "Spetsnaz soldiers, KGB agents, government bodyguards and police officers."[21] Since the instruction of body guards and police officers falls under the mandate of the Ministry of Interior Affairs, we can

---

[18] Vasiliev is described as 35 years old in 1995. See: https://web.archive.org/web/20001214174800/http:/www.russianm artialart.com/articles/brutal.html, accessed August 30, 2019. For the date, see:
https://www.facebook.com/systemavasiliev/posts/happy-birthday-to-vladimir-chief-instructor-at-systema-hq-toronto/935141879867089/, accessed Jan. 31, 2019
[19] "Vasiliev's exposure to the system came during his stint in the Russian army from 1977 to 1979." See: https://web.archive.org/web/20001214174800/http:/www.russianm artialart.com/articles/brutal.html, accessed August 30, 2019. On specialized training, see Vasiliev and Meredith, *Let Every Breath...*: 117
[20] *Systema for Life Podcast*, Episode 1, featuring Vladimir Vasiliev (Oct. 4, 2017)
[21] On his career as an instructor, see https://web.archive.org/web/20020603130403/http://russianmartial art.org/fightman.html, accessed Jan 1, 2017. For his age at the time, see Scott Meredith and Vladimir Vasiliev, *Edge: Secrets of the Russian Blade Masters* (Kindle Edition), Chapter Three, "My Body Wasn't Ready For It," First Paragraph, Location 392

assume that the MVD was the "different service" Vasiliev alludes to. If so, Vasiliev's transfer must have occurred in the very early 80s.

He reports that he first met Ryabko in Tver "over 30 years ago," in the "early 80s."[22] This is the time that Ryabko had also completed his own military service and joined the MVD. Testimony from Valentin Talanov—a former student of Ryabko who also lived in Tver—confirms this. He states that in 1982-1983 Ryabko had "just came out of his conscript service in the army."[23]

I imagine that Vasiliev transferred back to Tver and into the MVD in 1979. Then, in roughly 1983, after having himself eventually gained an instructorship, was introduced to Ryabko by a mutual acquaintance.[24]

Whenever the event occurred, we know that the two became friends very quickly.[25] What is less clear is what happened after that. Vasiliev asserts that he spent ten years overall in the Russian service.[26] Since that service began in 1977, his end date would have been roughly 1987. However, we have reason to believe that Vasiliev was an instructor with the MVD only until 1985.[27] Furthermore, we have his own testimony relating that he initially trained with Ryabko for only about a year-and-a-half.[28]

---

[22] http://www.russianmartialart.com/article_info.php?articles_id=74#.XWlOiShKjcs, accessed August 30, 2019
[23] http://en.systema-talanov.com/valentin_talanov, accessed September 5, 2019
[24] *Systema for Life Podcast*, Episode 1, featuring Vladimir Vasiliev (Oct. 4, 2017)
[25] https://warriorspathsystema.wordpress.com/2014/02/20/vladimir-vasiliev-formless-ferocity-blitz-martial-arts-magazine/, accessed May 17, 2019
[26] https://web.archive.org/web/20020603130403/http://russianmartialart.org/fightman.html, accessed August 30, 2019
[27] https://web.archive.org/web/20001214174800/http:/www.russianmartialart.com/articles/brutal.html, accessed August 30, 2019
[28] http://www.russianmartialart.com/article_info.php?articles_id=74#.XWlOiShKjcs, accessed August 30, 2019

From all of this we can perhaps say that sometime between 1983 and 1987, Vasiliev—for a relatively short period—received instruction from Ryabko. My own sense is that the training would have been between 1985 and 1987, prior to Vasiliev's departure from Russia, perhaps after he had finally moved away from the practice of Karate.

Whatever the truth, we know that Vasiliev emigrated from Russia to Canada in 1990, and that he would not see Ryabko in person again for another eight years after that.[29]

Vasiliev, speaking of his training prior to leaving Russia, states that, at that time, "Mikhail's teaching did not so much emphasize using breath to remove the punch or to protect ourselves. He mostly taught us to move the body away from the contact."[30] When asked about his reunion with Ryabko, whether the master had changed in the intervening years, Vasiliev remarked that "Mikhail had changed a lot... His movements were even more short and simple. He had more variety than in the past. He also became more spiritual and gained a lot of strength from there."[31] So there is definitely reason to suspect that Ryabko's training and philosophy had altered fundamentally between 1990 and the reunion of 1998.

Furthermore, in 1998, the Systema Headquarters website was simply called "Russian Martial Arts, By Vladimir Vasiliev and Michael Ryabko."[32] On the front page, Ryabko is described as having been "trained directly by Stalin's personal bodyguard." Clicking on the 'Background' tab brought you to a page that, after briefly listing a host of native Russian martial arts, goes into a description of Stalin's

---

[29]https://web.archive.org/web/20001215012400/http://www.russianmartialart.com/articles/systema.html, accessed August 30, 2019
[30] Scott Meredith and Vladimir Vasiliev: *Strikes: Body Meets Soul* (Russian Martial Art, 2015): 180
[31]http://www.russianmartialart.com/article_info.php?articles_id=74#.XWlVpShKjct, accessed August 30, 2019
[32]https://web.archive.org/web/19980623072037/http://www.russianmartialart.com/, accessed August 27, 2019

Falcons.[33] It asserts that these airbourne service members were Stalin's bodyguards and that

> "Close protection has always been the most vulnerable and challenging area in martial arts. The goal of Stalin's Falcons was to have a system that combined all the best components of the Russian System on all three levels of human abilities—the physical, the psychological and the psychic. And what is most important, to develop tactics that would not look like martial actions, tactics that are so subtle, that when they were applied it would be barely possible to see what happened and how."[34]

What's interesting to me about this advertisement is that it portrays Systema as the product of the Russian equivalent to the British Special Air Service (SAS) rather than as a singular folk tradition.[35] This is especially noteworthy to me when I recall that Viktor Suvorov's 1987 popular 'exposé' was titled *Spetsnaz: The Story Behind the Soviet SAS*. Furthermore, despite the mention of "psychic" abilities, I find it interesting that we are being led to view Systema as a strictly physical art, directed toward "martial actions."

The Systema Headquarters webpage would not make any reference to Russian knights of the tenth century or to Christian Orthodoxy until late 2003.[36] Nor would there be much mention of breathing before that time. The first

---

[33] I should note here that, since Stalin's Falcons was a name for Soviet aviators rather than Special Purpose Units, I do not know what to make of this. For a history of the term and its relationship with Stalinism, see K.E. Bailes, "Technology and Legitimacy: Soviet Aviation and Stalinism in the 1930s," *Technology and Culture*, Volume 17, Number 1 (1976)

[34] https://web.archive.org/web/19980623072057/http://www.russianmartialart.com/background.html, accessed August 30, 2019

[35] For more on Russian airborne units, see David Campbell, *Soviet Paratrooper vs. Mujahedeen Fighter: Afghanistan 1979-89* (Osprey, 2017)

[36] https://web.archive.org/web/20030807010657/http://russianmartialart.com/, accessed September 5, 2019

Systema Headquarters seminar that I can find which explicitly included breathing in its subject matter—"Complete Training on Breathing, Health & Conditioning"—would not be held until February 16 of 2002.[37]

Indeed, the primary focus of the art prior to 2003 seemed to be on 'natural movement.' For instance, second-hand testimony from Ryabko published on the Headquarters website in 2000 states that "the Russian System is one of the most effective because it relies on natural movements."[38] Similarly, *The Russian System Guidebook*, published in 1997, although it makes several very brief references to continuous breathing throughout, is primarily focused on communicating the virtues of natural movement.[39]

Furthermore, in the latter half of *Beyond the Physical*, which appears to have perhaps been recorded in September of 2001, Ryabko remarks that he and Vasiliev will have to produce a future video on breathing.[40] This statement is in response to the seminar participants' surprise and unfamiliarity with the subject.

As a matter of fact, early students of Vasiliev have commented on the physicality of early training sessions at Systema Headquarters, noting explicitly the lack of breathing. Headquarters' instructor Igor Ponizov calls those sessions "physically very intense," involving the repetition of similar movements and a respectful combative atmosphere.[41]

---

[37] https://web.archive.org/web/20020603124712/http://russianmartialart.com:80/html/seminars.html, accessed September 5, 2019
[38] https://web.archive.org/web/20001214202500/http://www.russianmartialart.com/articles/excerpts.html, accessed August 30, 2019
[39] Vasiliev, *The Russian System Guidebook* (Kindle Edition), Chapter Two, "Soviet Special Units Trainings," Location 211; Meredith and Vasiliev, *Edge*, Chapter Three, "Mikhail Could See to That Depth," Second Paragraph, Location 410
[40] For the original date and title of the seminar, see https://web.archive.org/web/20010710215519/http://www.russianmartialart.com/html/seminars.html, accessed September 5, 2019.
For Ryabko's comments, see Mikhail Ryabko, *Beyond the Physical* (Russian Martial Art, 2003)
[41] *Systema for Life Podcast*, Episode 16, featuring Igor Ponizov (January 19, 2018)

Vali Majd, an instructor now operating out of British Columbia who began with Vasiliev in 1995, reports that:

> "The warm ups were of course very different, I think during the first five years that I was there, there was no push-ups, there was no breathing, there was no squats, none of that stuff was part of the curriculum."[42]

My own instructor's testimony matches the above description:

> "In the early years of Systema, it was not as well defined. By that I mean there was little breath work, not a lot of push-ups or squat drills. We just came to class and studied self defence. Vladimir had so much energy and was very excited to show this art to whomever wanted to learn. It has changed over the years. If you really want to understand something in a masterful way, you have to go deeper. Re-understand what you know and grow. As the years went on, more details were discovered. It has been distilled year after year, with a finer and smoother product."[43]

From all of this, it seems safe to posit that between 1990 and 2000, before Ryabko first visited Toronto, the Systema that Vasiliev practiced was markedly different from what Ryabko would demonstrate upon their reunion, both in terms of content and ideology. I may be wrong, but the evidence seems to suggest that Systema Headquarters would not finish altering its curriculum until 2003, and would not fully disseminate it throughout the Systema community until 2006, the year that it published *Let Every Breath...: Secrets*

---

[42] *Systema for Life Podcast*, Episode 49, featuring Vali Majd (September 7, 2018)
[43] *Systema Voices*, Volume One, edited by Rob Poyton (Cutting Edge, 2018): 65

of the Russian Breath Masters and its accompanying DVD, *Systema Breathing: Secrets of the Russian Breath Masters.*

***

One thing that does not change in the history of Systema, however, is people's estimations of the founder. Those in the community who have spent time with Ryabko often speak of his gentle and pious demeanor. For example, long-time student Scott McQueen, who teaches in Japan, remarks that "one of my, kinda, biggest takeaways, even from that first seminar [in Russia], staying at Mikhail's house, and seeing how he interacted with his family, and his dedication and faith—that probably had a bigger impact on me than any of the martial stuff." McQueen also remarks on the fact that Ryabko maintains a private chapel in his backyard.[44] My own instructor, Manolakakis, is equally reverent of Ryabko's depth of character, often referring back to maxims and precepts that the master had imparted in conversation or in training.

Vasiliev's description of what first intrigued him about Ryabko is worth quoting as well. When asked about his early experiences with Systema, Vasiliev replies that

> "when I met Mikhail, and I was very surprised how he moves, uhm..., how say?.., ah, talk to people, speak with people... act with people, it was like, ah, so deep, usually you talk with the guy you already know who he is; with Mikhail it's like a big big hole, you cannot reach the bottom even. That's what I like about him."[45]

Even the art's co-founder is enamoured with Ryabko, seeing in him a benevolent mystery without solution, something that you can enter but never fathom.

---

[44] *Systema for Life Podcast*, Episode 16 featuring Scott McQueen (January 18, 2019)
[45] *Systema for Life Podcast*, Episode 1, featuring Vladimir Vasiliev (Oct. 4, 2017)

Ryabko, despite his sunken, sinister eyes, is always kind in interviews and demonstrations, smiling and working gently, showing a mountainous, dull ferocity only when appropriate.

When I see him working and read or hear from him in interviews, I think of a quote from journalist Anatol Lieven. Speaking about military culture in the late 90s, Lieven asserted that it "humiliates men, weakens them physically, and breaks them down without 'building them up.'"[46] This in turn makes me think of the *dedovshchina*, the infamous rule of the grandfathers among Russian soldiers. I may doubt the official origin story attached to his otherwise modern art, but I do not doubt that Ryabko is a man who, like many other soldiers, went through hell. Systema, I like to imagine, beyond any other cause, grew over time in response to that hell. In May of 2003, in a video directed towards future instructors, Ryabko remarks simply that the "main thing in war is not to become a beast."[47]

That said, his military experience would, to my mind, only account for half of Ryabko's attitude toward others. In addition to his military and martial arts training, there is within the man something else.

Vasiliev reports that Ryabko was raised in a rural farming community.[48] Perhaps it is my own prejudice which associates rural life with piety, but I imagine that the young and patriotic Ryabko possessed an affinity for the religion of the motherland. Keeping this faith to himself over the course of his military career, he endured his treatment with equanimity, keeping always in mind the teachings of his father and grandfather. Primed to embrace the nation's traditional faith, he enthusiastically endorsed and sought out the Russian Orthodox Church when it began to infiltrate the ranks of the Ministry of Interior Affairs at the end of the Cold War.

---

[46] Roger R. Reese, *The Soviet Military Experience: A History of the Soviet Army, 1917-1991* (Routledge, 2000): 150
[47] Mikhail Ryabko *Instructor Seminar* (Russian Martial Art, 2018)
[48] Meredith and Vasiliev, *Edge*, Chapter Three, "5,000 Cossacks," Second Paragraph, Location 446

Even if my conjecture is wrong, there is no denying that Ryabko is today a great champion of Russian Orthodox monasticism, which necessarily places him indirectly if not directly in contact with hesychast breath-centred religious practice.[49] Indeed, Brazilian instructor Nelson Wagner reports that Ryabko taught him to "breathe while praying."[50]

This connection to Orthodox monasticism, which would have been strengthened after 1990, might even account for the shift from "natural movement" to breathwork detected earlier. As Ryabko entered deeper into his own faith, he discovered somewhere in it an approach to religiosity which he could incorporate into his martial arts practice, disseminating his knowledge of breath-centred prayer to his students in Toronto and then outward to the world.

I propose that these two streams, Ryabko's experience with the military and his affinity for Orthodox monasticism, contribute more than anything else to the gentle expression of his spirit.

In his 2003 interview, Ryabko remarked that

> "there are a lot of positive things happening in Russian now. It is very possible that this sort of thing [the widespread growth of Systema] could happen. I am all for the rebirth and rebuilding of everything, in Russia, America, Europe, and Asia. I am for people, not against anything. I am for good. I am for justice. People are the same everywhere, in America, Canada, and Russia. Everyone has family and kids."[51]

---

[49] For awards see, http://systemaryabko.wixsite.com/systema/gratitudes, accessed September 5, 2019
[50] *Systema Voices*: 55
[51] https://web.archive.org/web/20160314103019/http://members.aikidojournal.com/private/interview-with-mikhail-ryabko/, accessed June 22, 2020

Ryabko, at least on paper, does not exclude anyone from practicing his art. We can imagine that this openness has contributed to the growth of Systema from a handful of small, unremarkable schools run out of basements and storefronts into a global subculture.

***

Which brings us to the final, contemporary phase of Systema's history: its commercialization and transformation into a brand identity.

I do not doubt the sincerity of Ryabko's faith or the power of his knowledge, nor do I doubt that of Vasiliev. Those qualities remain at the centre of the art. But I also cannot deny that the two men have built around that core a flourishing trade in products, novelties, and international seminars.

Systema is something that many individuals practice with devotion and intensity. They do so, however, wearing official brand-name Systema merchandise, replacing the ornamental costumes of traditional martial arts with camouflage pants and shirts that advertise the latest book or seminar.

In a way, you can detect the growth of this trend from Systema's earliest days. Systema Headquarters is a business that emerged at a unique moment in the development of global capitalism. VHS tapes and DVDs, and then YouTube, allowed Vasiliev and Ryabko to reach customers throughout the world, first through specialized distribution networks and martial arts shops and then through the internet.[52]

---

[52] Commenting on the role that YouTube videos play in the global BJJ community, sociologist Dale Spencer writes: "As a form of new social media, YouTube effectively democratizes the art of BJJ, making it available to anyone who has an Internet connection and computer. YouTube disseminates the display of techniques and users can encounter them, experiment with them and reflect on their usefulness in the art." See his "From Many Masters to Many Students: YouTube, Brazilian Jiu Jitsu, and Communities of Practice," *Journalism, Media and Cultural Studies* (June, 2014): 6

Coincidentally, the school in Toronto was founded in the same year that the first UFC was held (1993). An early self-defense video featuring Vasiliev, published by TRS in association with Systema Headquarters, co-starred Oleg Taktarov, the winner of UFC 6 in 1995. In fact, for a lengthy period of time, the early website even listed Taktarov as an instructor at the school.[53] Meredith, in an interview, notes that everyone at that time was looking for the next Brazilian Jiu-Jitsu.[54] Some might have been drawn to Systema as a consequence of its relation to the UFC brand.

Students who first stumbled upon Systema through these and similar audio-visual materials include Gene Smithson, Bratzo Barrena, Brad Scornavacco, Jason Priest, Edgars Cakuls, Sergey Makarenko, Pete Rogers, Matt Hill, Peter Annazone, and Rob Poyton.[55] Prior to the advent of Facebook and other social media, many of these individuals were no doubt also participants on Systema Headquarters' now defunct internet forum, sharing information and perspectives from around the world concerning the Russian Martial Art.[56]

In addition to the use of videos and digital forums, Systema Headquarters encourages its customers to buy branded t-shirts, training knives, whips, leather crosses, lanyards, patches, mugs, lunch bags, license plate frames, and even holographic stickers.[57] Everyone is invited to transform their body itself into an advertisement. Indeed, very often you can see these materials worn by dozens upon dozens of participants in footage taken from the constant string of large, and expensive, international seminars held annually.

**

---

[53] https://web.archive.org/web/19990429102915/http://www.russian martialart.com/, accessed February 23, 2020.
[54] *Systema for Life Podcast*, Episode 73, featuring Scott Meredith (February 22, 2019)
[55] See their respective *Systema for Life Podcast* interviews
[56] https://web.archive.org/web/19990912040623/http://www3.brave net.com/forum/show.asp?userid=rk104850, accessed August 27, 2019
[57] https://systemavasiliev.com/store/product-category/accessories/, accessed June 28, 2020

At first glance, Systema's embrace of a market-based globalized outreach strategy seems to be at odds with Ryabko's austere spirituality and the Stoic lifestyle of an elite soldier. However, when viewed in the context of the international wellness industry it is less surprising.

For example, religious scholar Andrea Jain admits that there appears to be a contradiction between the ideology of yoga, a posture practice which seeks to promote inner peace and universal harmony, and the billion-dollar industry surrounding it which shills yoga mats and branded outfits produced by overseas sweatshops as part of a globalized trade in goods and information. Jain argues, however, that this contradiction between ideology and practice is only apparent.

Nothing about yoga explicitly brings into question the structure of markets or of capitalism. Rather, it is an almost perfect consumer product, one that individuals can embrace in their quest to attain that most mythical of all states: well-being.[58] Yoga treats the body as a sacred object, setting it apart momentarily from the hustle and bustle of modernity so that it can be purified. Students are putting cash towards a ritual of atonement.[59]

In so many ways, the story of yoga is similar to the story Systema. Like yoga, it has become both a consumer identity and a means of repenting for and easing the strains of modern living. Furthermore, it was made possible by increased immigration and global freedom of movement. Its fundamental mystique—that of the Russian soldier providing secret knowledge from the East—even reflects the same Orientalist impulse which drove so many people to yoga in the early twentieth century.[60]

Systema remains the way of life developed early on by Ryabko and Vasiliev in response to their social and cultural

---

[58] Andrea Jain, *Selling Yoga: From Counterculture to Pop Culture* (Oxford University Press, 2014): 50, 75-78
[59] *Ibid*: 98, 109
[60] *Ibid*: 43

backgrounds, but now, for many people, that way comes with a t-shirt.

4. Know Yourself

At Fight Club where I train, Manolakakis has posted up on the walls, in unconscious emulation of the Oracle at Delphi, a number of instructions and focus words. Breathe, relax, courage, strength, focus, believe, have fun, and know yourself.

There are several reasons for me to have continued practicing Systema, but if I had to pick one reason above all others it would be the art's relationship with the commandment "know yourself." While I often find Systema's interpretation of the dictum frustrating—because it explicitly rejects intellect—I nevertheless remain intrigued; the historian in me loves when the past echoes in the present.

What is an ancient Greek commandment doing in a present-day fitness club?

In the original Greek, know yourself was gnōthi seauton; in Latin, it was nosce teipsum; and in Russian, it is poznai sebia. Regardless of the language used, the commandment is composed of an imperative verb, that is, a verb that commands you to do something, and a reflexive noun in the accusative case. You are being ordered to observe, gain information, become familiar, or be certain regarding one thing and one thing only: you yourself.

Pierre Hadot, viewing the phrase in the context of ancient philosophy, asserts that, although "it is difficult to be sure of the original meaning of 'know yourself,' this much is clear: it invites us to establish a relationship of the self to the self, which constitutes the foundation of every spiritual exercise."[1] In other words, whatever the original command's meaning, to be told to know yourself in ancient philosophy was to be invited to treat yourself as the subject of an inquiry. And, as Michel Foucault shows, the act of self-inquiry is often the

---

[1] Pierre Hadot, *Philosophy as a Way of Life: Spiritual Exercises from Socrates to Foucault*, edited by Arnold Davidson (Blackwell Publishing, 1995): 90

same as the act of self-discipline.[2] When you treat yourself as the subject of an inquiry, you subjectivize yourself, transforming your body into a subject in the legal sense of the term, like being subject to a king.

For Systema students, know yourself—as it was with ancient philosophical schools—is a command to treat yourself as the subject of an inquiry for the purpose of transforming yourself *into* a subject. Komarov, in his *Systema Manual*, echoes these ancient ideas.

> "It is important to know that *every exercise in Systema is, first and foremost, a mirror, in which we can carefully examine ourselves from a new angle and see our flaws, shortcomings, tensions, and imperfections.* Second, any Systema exercise is an instrument to correct and rebuild us."[3]

However, unlike in the ancient world, the focus of Systema is not on the ideas of the mind but rather on the movements and emotional states of the body. Through observation of the body and its emotions while in conflict, the student of Systema seeks to smooth out the edges of their exterior with the belief that this will imbue them with a new interiority, a new identity, a new character.

Systema directs you to know yourself not as a new Socrates, skilled in contemplation and dialogue, but as an equanimous warrior monk, skilled in patient attention to the present moment.

---

[2] "...the text says it: Those who govern should also be those who philosophize, who practice philosophy. What, for Plato, is this practice of philosophy? Before all else, essentially and fundamentally, this practice of philosophy is a way for the individual to constitute himself as a subject of a certain mode of being." See Michel Foucault, *The Government of Self and Others: Lectures at the College de France, 1982-1983*, translated by Graham Burchell (Palgrave Macmillan, 2001): 294-296

[3] Konstantin Komarov, *Systema Manual*, translated by Dimitri Trufanov (Systema Headquarters, 2014): 23 (emphasis in original)

***

Before we get into a close reading of Systema's uses of know yourself, it is worth reviewing the interpretations that proliferated in Greek and Latin literature. There are at least five types that are relevant to our discussion. The first and likely original meaning of know yourself would have been "know your faults and weakness as a mortal." Citing the research of preeminent classicist Walter Burkert, Ursula Renz reports that "when the inscription "Gnothi seauton" was fixed at the temple of Apollo, it was meant to remind the reader, who was about to enter the temple dedicated to one of the most sublime gods, of his belonging to the category of merely mortal beings."[4] It was intended to humble those entering a holy site.

The second interpretation can be found in Xenophon's *Cyropaedia* and Plato's *Philebus*, where know yourself is taken to mean "know your measure," that is, probe and accept the extent of your own abilities.[5] The commandment directs readers to not think themselves greater than they are, to not over-estimate their wealth, appearance, and character. By accepting your status in life, your given place and given qualities, you bring a degree of peace to your life.

The third interpretation is closely related to the first but the emphasis is on abstractions rather than concrete realities— "know the limits of knowledge." In Plato's *Charmides*, for instance, knowledge of the limits of knowledge itself is key to the development of internal harmony and self-control. Here know yourself is a command to understand what is knowable and what cannot be known so that you can bring the appetites of the body and the emotions of the mind into

---

[4] The interpretations suggested are: "Know, oh man, that you are not a god," and "know thyself, man, as a mortal being, in your mortality." See Ursula Renz, "Introduction," in *Self-Knowledge: A History*, edited by Ursula Renz (Oxford University Press, 2017): 13
[5] Eliza Gregory Wilkins, *"Know Thyself" in Greek and Latin Literature* (University of Chicago Libraries, 1917): 15-17

a rational balance.⁶ Socrates, who was named in an early dialogue as the wisest of Athenians for having known himself, was often depicted probing the limits of his knowledge, questioning his interlocutors, rarely satisfied with a given answer. And, indeed, many of the answers Socrates received tended to throw his universe into further confusion, leaving him to wonder if he'd ever rightly understand anything at all. At the same time, he was consistently depicted as a man capable of extreme acts of contemplation and self-control, even standing unprotected from the elements, oblivious to the cold. ⁷

Along the same lines, the fourth interpretation denies our individual capacity for self-knowledge. The ancient Roman physician Galen claimed, like the French Moralists of the seventeenth century who would follow, that you cannot be trusted to evaluate your own abilities— your self-love turns too easily into self-flattery. Only when you ask others to tell you what they see, and order them to report truthfully, can you gain a more accurate account of your personality and abilities.⁸ It was in this spirit that the Roman statesman Plutarch, in his *How to tell a Flatterer from a Friend*, contrasted the truth-telling friend from the misleading flatterer. "For the flatterer always takes a position over and against the maxim 'know thyself,' by creating in every man deception towards himself and ignorance both of himself and

---

⁶ See Peter Adamson, *Classical Philosophy: A History of Philosophy Without Any Gaps*, Volume One (Oxford University Press, 2014): 109-116; Tobias Myers "Reflection I: Does Homer's Odysseus Know Himself," in *Self-Knowledge: A History*, edited by Ursula Renz (Oxford University Press, 2017): 27-32
⁷ Raymond Guess, *Changing the Subject: From Socrates to Adorno* (Harvard University Press, 2017): Ch. 1
⁸For Galen, see James Hankinson, "Actions and Passions: Affection, Emotion, and Moral Self-Management in Galen's Philosophical Psychology," in *Passions & Perceptions: Studies in Hellenistic Philosophy of Mind*, edited by Jacques Brunschwig and Martha C. Nussbaum (Cambridge University Press, 1993): 199-201. For the French Moralists, see Aaron Garrett, "Self-Knowledge and Self-Deception in Modern Moral Philosophy," in *Self-Knowledge: A History*, edited by Ursula Renz (Oxford University Press, 2017): 172-175

of the good and evil that concerns himself."[9] In this both Galen and Plutarch no doubt borrowed from Aristotle, who reasoned, while thinking about the Delphic oracle, that self-knowledge required a friend or 'second self.'[10] Here the quest for self-knowledge becomes a cooperative goal.

Finally, a fifth interpretation takes know yourself to mean "know your own soul." This is explicitly the case in pseudo-Plato's *First Alcibiades*. In that forged letter the argument is that if one accepts the existence of an immortal or at least immaterial soul then knowledge of the self must regard something beyond the material realm. Those who wished to know their own self therefore needed to reorient the mind and its imagination away from concern for the body and towards concern for what is simple, unified, and unchanging in the cosmos.[11] This interpretation was taken up later by the Neoplatonists and, through them, the early Christians. For example, the prototypical Christian monk, Anthony of the Desert writes that "Jesus knows himself in his spiritual essence, for he who knows himself also knows the dispensation of the Creator, and what he does for his creatures"[12] Know yourself was here a directive to perform, like Christ in the desert, an act of self-denial that would reveal the order of the universe and the benevolent activities of God himself.

***

Having reviewed a small portion of the history of know yourself, it's worth returning once again to Systema Headquarters' website. There we read that knowing yourself means more than knowing where you are physically strong and weak; it also involves seeing "the full extent of our

---

[9] Daniel J. Kapust, *Flattery and the History of Political Thought: That Glib and Oily Art* (Cambridge University Press, 2018): 6
[10] Christopher Shields, "Aristotle's Requisite of Self-Knowledge" in *Self-Knowledge: A History*, edited by Ursula Renz (Oxford University Press, 2017): 50
[11] Eliza Gregory Wilkins, *"Know Thyself" in Greek and Latin Literature*: 60-61
[12] David Brakke, *Demons and the Making of the Monk: Spiritual Combat in Early Christianity* (Harvard University Press, 2006): 18

limitations—to see how proud and weak we really are." Such insight "allows us to gain the true strength of spirit that comes from humility and clarity in seeing the purpose of our life." According to the advertisement, such an interpretation is found in the tradition of Russian Orthodox Christianity. The page states that all events, good or bad, occur for a single, ultimate reason, "to create the best possible conditions for each person to understand himself."[13]

The fundamental assumption, you'll note, is that humanity is a profoundly delusional species. Not only are we weak, but—in an act of pride—we deny our weakness to ourselves. Accepting this truth and believing it allows us to access something called 'strength of spirit' and to perceive a larger purpose to our existence. Indeed, through self-knowledge, the cosmos itself is revealed to possess an elaborate design, one that encourages us to face our weaknesses and overcome our delusions.

Systema is offered as a method of kickstarting this process, allowing us to begin to exorcise the delusions which limit perception.

> "Training in Systema lets the person see his own egotism and other weaknesses and gives him ammunition to overcome them. A humble person devotes his life to fighting the evil in his heart and constantly asks God to help him with that. In reward for his hard work and resulting humility, God gives him this amazing gift of peace, joy and absence of resentment no matter what happens."

Once we have begun to see clearly, we become humble, that is, locked into a state of perpetual spiritual combat with the evils in our heart, petitioning higher powers for assistance so that we might overcome our flawed and delusion-prone

---

[13] https://www.russianmartialart.com/whatis.php, accessed September 26, 2016

nature. Peace, joy, and the absence of resentment are by-products of such unceasing prayer.

Because of Systema's explicit connection to Orthodox Christianity, I am reminded of the writings of Theophan the Recluse. "True self-knowledge is to see one's own defects and weaknesses so clearly that they fill our whole view. And mark this—the more you see yourself at fault and deserving of every censure, the more you will advance."[14] For Theophan, humanity was so deeply flawed that the only reliable pathway to holiness was to understand and believe wholeheartedly that you are at root guilty of some unspoken transgression. Towards this end Theophan, echoing *Matthew 7:18-20*, encouraged his readers to keep their mind's eye on the heart and to look closely at what comes forth from it. If the products of the heart are good, let them be; if they are evil, kill them at once; "in this way, learn to know yourself."[15] Here the procedure is to assume guilt at all moments, and to scrutinize every thought and action, seeking out bad results so that they can be eliminated.

As mentioned before, Theophan the Recluse was a hesychast who believed in the purifying efficacy of the Jesus Prayer. To quote again from the nineteenth-century Russian monk:

> "the practice of the Jesus Prayer is simple. Stand before the Lord with the attention in the heart, and call to Him: 'Lord Jesus Christ, Son of God, have mercy on me!' The essential part of this is not in the words, but in faith, contrition, and self-surrender to the Lord. With these feelings one can stand before the Lord even without any words, and it will still be prayer."[16]

---

[14] Theophan the Recluse, in *The Art of Prayer: An Orthodox Anthology*, translated by E. Kadloubovsky and E.M. Palmer, edited by Timothy Ware (Faber and Faber, 1966): 222
[15] *Ibid*: 229
[16] *Ibid*: 89

In the Hesychast tradition, the heart is symbolic not of the soul, but of the entire complex of mind and body.[17] The act of prayer in this tradition was thus a whole-body experience in which one sought, above all other emotions, to embody faith and submission to God, as well as remorse for sins. One could measure progress in this activity through the sensation of what Theophan calls warmth of the heart; "prayer of the mind changes into prayer of the heart, or rather into prayer of the mind in the heart: its appearance coincides with the birth of warmth of the heart."[18] This warmth of the heart manifests itself as the concentration of all thoughts into a single whole, completely directed toward God.[19]

As with nineteenth-century monastic practice, for Systema practitioners the act of knowing yourself is two-pronged: on the one hand, it is an act of observation and selection regarding your actions; on the other, it is a quest to embody an emotional matrix. You are not being asked to know yourself as a self, that is, as a collection of memories, ideas, and opinions, but rather to know yourself in the guise of a specific character, forsaking much of your conscious identity. Observing yourself, you prune away or cut off those things that are evil so that only the good remains. At the same time, you focus the entirety of your being towards God and the atonement of sins. Doing so will produce a complete emotional realignment.

In all of this we can hear the echoes of "know your faults and weaknesses as a mortal," "know your measure," and "know your soul." You are humbling yourself before a deity, accepting your position and capacities, and seeking to access feelings and information from an immaterial realm.

Still, at this point, it remains unclear how exactly Systema as it is practiced fits into this tradition. Some questions which remain unanswered are: What is good? What is evil? How

---

[17] Kallistos Ware, "'My Helper and My Enemy': The Body in Greek Christianity," in *Religion and the Body*, edited by Sarah Coakley (Cambridge University Press, 1997): 100
[18] Theophan the Recluse, in *The Art of Prayer: An Orthodox Anthology*: 72
[19] *Ibid*: 159

does the process of identification work? How exactly do you kill an evil product once you have recognized it? What's the process here?

***

A short article published under Vasiliev's name in January 2011, entitled "Are You Really Training?," goes a long way towards answering those questions.

> "Your partner does an *unfair* move towards you, for example: he responds to your light strike with a hard and painful one. And then you get angry.
>
> Or your partner is a bit arrogant or slow to learn, and you get irritated.
>
> Or, you find your moves work very well, and that makes you proud of yourself.
>
> Or someone praises you and vanity starts to creep in.
>
> I see this happening every class. In this case, your real training time might be only a few minutes out of the entire session...
>
> ...The focus of Systema is different - you need to <u>understand yourself</u>. What does that mean? Watch constantly what is it that interferes with your calm, objective and continuous movement.
>
> Uncontrolled emotions are detrimental to effective work. These feelings come in a subtle way and unnoticeably begin to dominate and eat away at your strength. We must be vigilant. Step one is to be aware of these weaknesses; step two is to try to overcome them through breathing, understanding, changing the attitudes and

the movements. Then we gain true strength and skill."[20]

Once again, we read language that is highly monastic. Here, however, Vasiliev offers readers a concise description of Systema's methodology rather than an outline of its larger theological underpinnings and spiritual aims.

Systema is a method of modifying the body so that its movements are uninfluenced by feelings or opinions. Such movements, according to Vasiliev, take the form of an uninterrupted, unbroken whole. Here there are two ideas. The first is that this idealized form of movement is real and possible, and the second is that feelings of anger, irritation, pride, and vanity negatively affect our capacity to move in an idealized way. If we accept these two propositions, then we must watch ourselves—our feelings and movements—for expressions of harmful emotions.[21] When those types of emotions are detected, we ought to deploy Systema, that is, breathing techniques designed to cleanse the body of anger, irritation, pride, and vanity so that we no longer think and move in a way that impedes the expression of idealized motion.

Later in the same article, Vasiliev writes, "As we know, memorized techniques often let you down in real unrehearsed confrontations, for example, if your arm is broken or if you are in a confined space. Whereas, if you can control your emotions and study movement, you will be capable of solving any problem in a multitude of ways." True strength and skill is, according to this perspective, the ability to engage in physical conflict from a position of extreme

---

[20] http://www.russianmartialart.com/article_info.php?articles_id=48 #.XLoBlehKjIU, accessed April 19, 2019 (emphasis in the original)
[21] Compare Vasiliev's instruction to "watch constantly" with Hesychios the Priest on the quality of watchfulness and holiness. "Watchfulness is a spiritual method which, if sedulously practiced over a long period, completely frees us with God's help from impassioned thoughts, impassioned words, and evil action." See Hesychos the Priest, "On Watchfulness and Holiness," in *Philokalia*, Volume One, edited and translated by G.E.H Palmer, Philip Sharrard, and Kallistos Ware (Farrar, Straus and Giroux, 1983): 162

disadvantage, without reference to engineered techniques or memorized patterns of motion.

Merging Vasiliev's description of know yourself with that given on the website, we can say that, in Systema, good and evil are not chosen actions, not moral choices as such, but rather emotional and bodily states. If your motion is smooth and unbroken, and you are not feeling anger, irritation, vanity, or pride, then you are exhibiting goodness. If your motion is choppy and you can't stand the people around you, then you are exhibiting evil. The primary means of killing off emotional and bodily evil is through breathing, prayer, and the reform of movement. Systema's founders are claiming, so far as I can tell, that if you make this ethic your own, that is, if you know yourself, you will be rewarded with the capacity to solve complex problems in otherwise highly stressful situations and experience the joy that comes from freedom from disturbing emotions.

***

Surprisingly, given the centrality of know yourself in the practice of Systema, Vasiliev does not often make use of the commandment publically. He remarks at the very end of the *Breath for Internal Control* DVD—almost in an offhand manner—that the exercises demonstrated reveal our weaknesses to us so that we can better know ourselves.[22] This statement, short as it is, is consistent with what we have noted above.

In *Strikes: Soul Meets Body*, when describing the attitude that we ought to take in a conflict, he states that "you need to know how not to be there to please or impress, not to be pressured. You're ether there for yourself or not at all. So don't be ruled by your emotions, 'disappear from yourself'. We could also phrase it the exact opposite: 'find yourself', 'know yourself'."[23] As the above discussion would lead us to expect, for Vasiliev, the call to know yourself refers above all

---

[22] Vladimir Vasiliev, *Breath for Internal Control* DVD (Russian Martial Art, 2014)
[23] Vladimir Vasiliev and Scott Meredith, *Strikes: Soul Meets Body* (Russian Martial Art, 2018): 57

at your emotional state. When confronted with conflict, we are often placed on a stage, in front of an audience. The goal of Systema's emotional and bodily realignment is to teach you how to act as if you are not being watched by anyone other than yourself and God.

What interests me about the description offered here is the equation of disappear from yourself and know yourself. In explicit terms the goal of training is to abnegate the interior self, to push it out of your vision, so that you can focus exclusively on the external self, the agitations of feeling and movement. There is nothing in here about memory or opinion or understanding in any abstract metaphysical sense. Thought does not come into it—only activity and feeling.

But, if the goal of Systema's martial arts training is meant to focus on the self to the exclusion of others, what do we say about the fact that we have so many training partners? After all, Konstantin Komarov, in *Systema Manual*, describes the ideal training scenario as one involving a master who molds you into the image of Systema, making you repeat painful exercises and actions for a long time, "dedicating a lot of time to partner work, and constantly correcting mistakes."[24] Individuals can train alone if they must, but Systema is at its best when it's a communal exercise, one in which students work and learn under the direction of an experienced master.

A common simile that you'll hear from Systema instructors is that a hard floor is like a good friend. We "go to the ground" a lot in Systema, evading strikes or negotiating the aftermath of takedowns. Since this can be quite painful if the floor is hard, we have to be careful and in control during our descent. In this way the hardness of the floor is like a good friend, telling you what you are doing wrong.[25] It is precisely the same with partner work. If you are not careful or in control, you're likely to get yourself hurt or to experience an emotional disturbance.

---

[24] Konstantin Komarov, *Systema Manual* (Systema Headquarters, 2014): 17
[25] Vasiliev and Meredith, *Strikes: Soul Meets Body*: 178, 180-181

Another moment when Vasiliev makes reference to the commandment know yourself is in relation to strikes: "... The static training for taking strikes is a way to know yourself. You need to truly understand that you're afraid."[26] Such an exercise cannot be performed without a partner. Nor would it be possible to identify negative emotions such as vanity, pride, or anger without partners. We saw this in Vasiliev's "Are You Really Training?" but had not commented on it. When a partner does something and an emotion emerges, you're being shown something: that you are angry or vain or prideful. In many respects, the social interaction between you and your partner *is* the training.

And yet, for all of that, in Systema, know yourself remains a personal experience. You are directed and you are inspired and you are made to suffer with others, but, in the end, you are to do so alone, or more than alone—without even yourself.

***

Looking at Ryabko's words on the subject reveals that the ultimate goal of this process, even in group work, is strict bodily and emotional attention to the present moment.

In a joint interview with Issho Fujita, a Zen priest, Ryabko offers a revealing statement. When Tokyo-based Systema instructor Takahide Kitagawa asks Fujita about his view of Systema as a religious practitioner, the priest comments on Ryabko's Orthodox rosary, the *chotki* that he had held in hand during the seminar. The seminar was devoted to the use of a spear. Ryabko was holding the spear in one hand and the rosary in the other. Fujita sees in this mix of the physical and spiritual a balanced coordination of body and psyche.

Elaborating further, Fujita remarks that through this coordination it is possible to "respond to enemies' attacks without disturbing our balance, while paying attention to those around us in order to avoid hurting them inadvertently." He sees in this attitude a "very religious kind

---

[26] *Ibid*: 88

of living." Because of this balance, Ryabko can "find moment by moment anew the most natural way of being." Systema does not employ force, it does not make plans; its paradigmatic practitioner, Ryabko, is simply waiting, open to the possibilities of the moment. The goal is "not doing what we think; it is just being in that state [of waiting openness]." Ryabko, hearing this, responds simply that he agrees, but then adds cryptically that, while everyone is unique, we all share commonalities; "the first thing to do is to know yourself, that is, to see in what direction you are heading."[27]

We might say that for Ryabko know yourself equates to going with the flow or being in the moment. The person who knows their self is, as in the Zen tradition, a hollow reed through which reality flows; there is no interiority, no thought as such, just open, unmediated acceptance and reaction to that which is presented.

If this is true, then it is consistent with what we know of Christian monasticism. Hadot reports that for early Christian monks "attention to the present is simultaneous control of one's thoughts, acceptance of the divine will, and purification of one's intentions with regard to others."[28] Ryabko, one assumes, has gained his abilities through the abnegation of self which I described above—through the elimination of emotions such as pride and vanity, through the reform of movements, and through prayer. In the Russian Orthodox tradition, this state of being is referred to as inner prayer.

> "Inner prayer means standing with the mind in the heart before God, either simply living in His presence, or expressing supplication, thanksgiving, and glorification. We must acquire the habit of always being in communion with God, without any image,

---

[27] https://shimoa.wixsite.com/kotsu/single-post/2016/06/17/Stray-notes-about-SYSTEMA-Dialog-between-Mikhail-Ryabko-and-Issho-Fujita-Systema-as-Seen-by-a-Zen-Priest, accessed May 25, 2019
[28] Hadot, *Philosophy as Way of Life*: 132

any process of reasoning, any perceptible movement of thought."[29]

Knowing yourself in Systema is a means—but not the only means—through which you can enter into a state of inner prayer. Its training drills work to remind you of your mortality and to reveal your measure; the inclusion of partners serves to help you overcome your own self-flattery; and the frequent echoes of Christian monasticism encourage you to consider yourself as part of a cosmic whole. In the state of inner prayer, your mind existing throughout the body, your emotions settling into a benevolent apathy, you become open and patient with the world, able to find your place at any given moment, both in peace and in conflict.

Ryabko's embrace of this ideology is confirmed elsewhere in the interview. When asked about the role of self-confidence and external support, Systema's founder responds that,

> "I believe in God. I believe that God exists and he created everything, so he will not forsake me. I also believe in the words in the Gospel, "He who believes will be saved." In Japan, some people served the shogun. Similarly, one can serve the God. You get money by serving the shogun, and you are protected and get other benefits by serving the God. On the other hand, believing in yourself starts by knowing yourself. By knowing where and with whom you are, and what your existence means, you get confidence in yourself.[30]

---

[29] Theophan the Recluse, *The Art of Prayer: An Orthodox Anthology*: 71
[30] https://shimoa.wixsite.com/kotsu/single-post/2016/06/17/Stray-notes-about-SYSTEMA-Dialog-between-Mikhail-Ryabko-and-Issho-Fujita-Systema-as-Seen-by-a-Zen-Priest, accessed September 6, 2019

At the core of Systema is the belief in an ordered and benevolent universe, in which self-knowledge is directly linked to divine revelation.

***

If we accept the conclusions of the first three chapters of this book—that Systema is a remnant of ancient philosophical ways of life that has been couched in the terms and practices of nineteenth and early twentieth century physical culture, militant nationalism, and popular religion—then we should not be surprised with Fujita's evaluation of the art.

The rhetoric of Christianity enables this coordination. Biblical passages such as *Ephesians 6:11-17, Isaiah 59:17, Wisdom 5:17-22,* and *Luke 11:21-*22 described faith as an armour and a sword to be used against evil. Monastics inherited this imagery and used it in their own writings, conceiving of their asceticism as a spiritual combat against demonic forces. In Evagrios Ponticos' *On Prayer* we read: "The warfare between us and the demons is waged solely on account of spiritual prayer. For prayer is extremely hateful and offensive to them, whereas it leads us to salvation and peace."[31] Theophan echoes this sentiment several centuries later.

> "Prepare yourself like an experienced fighter, and even if you see a sudden apparition do not be shaken; and should you see a sword drawn against you, or a torch thrust into your face, do not be alarmed. Should you see even some loathsome and bloody figure, do not panic; but stand fast, holding firm to your faith, and you will be more resolute in confronting your enemies."[32]

In the past, demonic possession was understood to manifest itself as emotional turmoil and even madness. Removing

---

[31] Evagrios Ponticos, "On Prayer," in *Philokalia*, Volume One, edited and translated by G.E.H Palmer, Philip Sharrard, and Kallistos Ware (Farrar, Straus and Giroux, 1983): 61
[32] *Ibid*: 66

damaging emotions such as vanity, pride, and anger, and replacing them with a reasoned balance of bodily appetites and human desires was thought to return men and women to a state of being like that which existed before the Fall of Man.[33] Ryabko, in holding the spear in one hand and the rosary in another, is symbolically enacting this rhetoric. He is reminding himself of his own state of perpetual spiritual combat.

Ancient philosophers, prior to the advent of Christianity, had also compared their practice with the training of soldiers and athletes. In Stoicism, for instance, the art of living is compared to the art of wrestling. The philosopher needed to be on guard and sure-footed against the difficult events of the world. Epictetus, writing about the progress of philosophers, explains that

> "The signs of a person making progress are these: criticizing nobody, praising nobody, blaming nobody, accusing nobody, and saying nothing about oneself to indicate being someone or knowing something. Whenever such a person is frustrated or impeded, he accuses himself. If he's complimented, he laughs to himself at the one paying the compliment, and if he's criticized, he doesn't defend himself...He doesn't care if he appears simple-minded or ignorant. In a word, he keeps watch on himself as though he were his own enemy plotting an attack."[34]

Early Christian monks, when they drew upon the imagery of warfare from the Hebrew Scriptures, paired their self-conception as soldiers of God with the self-conception of the philosophers, thinking of themselves as philosophers of Christ. When these monks did so, however,—and this is a subtle but important distinction to grasp—it was in a stable

---

[33] Richard Greenfield, *Traditions of Belief in Late Byzantine Demonology* (Adolf M. Hakkert, 1988): 90-97
[34] Epictetus, *How To Be Free: An Ancient Guide to the Stoic Life*, translated by A.A. Long (Princeton University Press, 2018): 85-87

and isolated environment, away from the conflicts of everyday life, living with other monks who were also engaged in fasting, prayer, and meditation on Scripture. In contrast, the ancient philosophers lived in the world, engaged in politics, fought in wars, and raised families. They opened themselves up to the world, taking on its difficulties. With monks it was very different; their training was internalized. They needed to stand sure-footed yes, but only against their own psychic interior, where demons would attack directly.[35]

Systema, despite its monastic roots, marks a sort of regression from the spiritual athleticism of the Christian monastics to the athleticism of the ancient philosophers. Like them, the students of Systema are athletes of the event, of the contest, rather than athletes of a strictly inner landscape.

***

Having tried to understand Systema's conception of know yourself on its own terms, let's take a step back now and isolate more precisely what's going on. What sort of self-knowledge does the practice of Systema provide us with?

There are at least three kinds of knowledge. The first kind is direct experience. In a martial arts context we would say that it is the sort of knowledge you would receive from your first time wrestling. You are engaged directly with another subject without reference to a technique or method of inquiry. At the end you can find yourself able to say: "I know now what it is like to wrestle" or "I have direct experience with wrestling." But beyond that, you probably couldn't say anything about wrestling itself. That would be the second type: propositional knowledge, the knowledge *that* something is the case.

"I know that the speed of light is very fast," and "I know that if you do x then y will result" are examples of propositional knowledge. We can also call this experimental knowledge, propositions gained through

---

[35] Michel Foucault, *The Hermeneutics of the Subject: Lectures at the College de France, 1981-1982*, translated by Graham Burchell (Palgrave Macmillan, 2001): 321-322

trial, error, and observation of outcomes, or from thorough evaluations—"I know that when applying an arm bar I need to isolate the arm in a particular way and be mindful of the position of my opponent's thumb so that I may find the correct biomechanical lever."

This leads us to the third kind of knowledge: know-how, the knowledge of how something is done. In the case of know-how, you possess the ability to perform an action, such as applying an arm bar, but may not have the ability to explain to others your method. For that you would need the know-how of teaching.[36]

With these distinctions in mind, we can say that Systema provides direct knowledge of bodily and emotional states and also know-how regarding the manipulation of those states. It does not often, however, provide propositional knowledge. Holding your breath and going through the motions of a push up, for instance, will only provide you with direct knowledge of the bodily and emotional state which results from the exercise. Yes, you may be able to say afterwards *that* holding your breath causes you to panic, but you won't be able—without conscious measuring and evaluation—to say afterwards *that* your body went into panic after 15.5 seconds or *that* panic involves the release of internal chemicals or any other specific propositional claims.

These three types of knowledge—direct, propositional, and know-how—are also applicable to the question of self-knowledge. But, if so, what are the objects of such knowledge? If you have direct experience of yourself, for instance, what sorts of things might yourself consist of?

Philosopher Ursula Renz isolates four basic types of self-knowledge. The first type regards your perceptions and sensations and passing thoughts; the second, your attitudes toward the world, including your beliefs, preferences, values, and goals; the third, your own characteristics and behaviour;

---

[36] For more on the distinctions between direct knowledge, propositional knowledge, and know-how, see Guess, *Changing the Subject: From Socrates to Adorno*: 17-18

and the fourth, your being subject to the human condition.[37] Use of these distinctions allows us to speak more precisely about the sort of knowledge that the practice of Systema produces.

Systema provides direct knowledge of bodily sensations and movements, and direct knowledge of attitudes, preferences, and behaviour. However, this latter form of knowledge is described exclusively in the idiom of Christian monasticism, that is, within the definition of vanity, pride, anger, humility, and joy. There is, for example, no explicit role for emotions such as wonder or disgust. Nor, we should say, are there any positive connotations given to the emotions of vanity, pride, or anger; they tend to be understood purely in the negative.

Systema teaches you how to detect in yourself the expression of negative emotions, how to expunge negative emotions from your actions, and—ideally—how to replace them with preferred emotions and movements.

In this sense Systema is both profound and extremely limited. It is profound because its practice amounts to the reformation of your emotional and bodily habits and thus a large portion of your character itself. A life without vanity, pride, and anger lived in the spirit of humility and joy is nothing to sneeze at.

At the same time, Systema as a regimen of physical and emotional training does not provide one with the skills to interrogate the full range of our human perceptions, or the means to identify and categorize thoughts, or to isolate preferences, values, and goals, or to evaluate character outside of the monastic idiom, or to empathize more completely with other members of our species. Nothing in Systema requires us to read novels or listen to music or otherwise engage with the humanities or arts. Nothing in Systema requires science or reason. Rather, every human experience and interaction is conceived of as an ascetic performance, nothing more and nothing less.

---

[37] Ursula Renz, "Introduction," *Self-Knowledge: A History*: 9-11

All that matters is the way of life—knowing your measure, knowing that you are mortal, knowing yourself through experience in a community, and knowing that you are soul.

For this reason it is appropriate that Ryabko was paired with a Zen priest in the above interview. Because it seems to me that Systema suffers from the same weakness of intellect that religious scholar Dale Wright finds in the practice of Zen Buddhism.

Wright explains that because Zen training is so heavily focused on the submission to skilled teachers, physical discipline, ritual procedure, calming meditation, silence, *koans*, and "direct perception without conceptual mediation," with the aim of producing mindfulness, endurance, self-discipline, courage, presence, and focus, there is no room for what Zen students would call "skill-in-means" abilities regarding complex moral issues or other abstract matters.[38] Zen, like Systema, "does not include the skills of reflection, conversation, reasoning, debating, organizing, or planning."[39] Indeed, as Wright goes on to argue, "one of the great dangers to the Zen tradition is its ever-present temptation to be disdainful of conceptual thinking" or even teaching that thought is a sickness.[40]

I cannot speak to others' experiences, but I have heard on more than one occasion from my own instructor comments to the effect that abstract thought and a lack of present-mindedness are societal evils.

None of this is to say that Systema practitioners are somehow *incapable* of abstract, metaphysical inquiry, or that they do not prize these things personally. My point—and this is what so often frustrates me with Systema—is that nothing in what it teaches will give someone the skill to engage in higher order thought regarding society or ethics. You are being taught to look at your body and its emotions, to modify your

---

[38] Dale Wright, *What is Buddhist Enlightenment?* (Oxford University Press, 2016): 96
[39] *Ibid*: 103
[40] *Ibid*: 100

behaviour, and to remain in the present moment without thought. That is all.

As a way of life, Systema can be hostile to intellect.

***

I am in no way a Christian. Nor do I have any use for the concept of God, other than as something interesting to think about. But—it seems to me—anyone who wishes to get to the core of what know yourself means in the context of Systema needs to understand where the art is coming from. This is particularly so if we wish to understand the origins of Ryabko's and Vasiliev's well-regarded bodily and emotional control. If I am correct, then what I have described above is the essence of their way of life and an important source of their focus and precision.

In order to wear the mask of the Systema master, you too need to know yourself through observation and reform, the elimination of vanity, pride, and anger, the embrace of peace and joy, and disregard for propositional knowledge. Like the monk, you must stand with your mind in your heart in the presence of God and like an ancient philosopher you must do so in the hustle and bustle of the wider world. This mix of spiritual and secular training will balance your emotions and smooth out the actions of your body, leaving you open and waiting for whatever will be to be.

Sometimes, when I am training at Fight Club, silently suffering through a demanding exercise, I look at the commandment to know yourself posted high up on the wall and I try to remember everything I've written here.

5. The Nervous System(a)

It probably wasn't the first time, but it was the first time that I'd noticed. My instructor had us enact a little drama.[1] It changed everything I had thought about Systema.

Manny selects a student from across the room. His name is Jason. By this time, Jason has been a member of the club for several years. I watch as he begins to come toward Manny with slow and medium-speed strikes and grabs.

As Manny speaks, he moves subtly from Jason's advances, pushing into his structure; striking him with precision to the face, chest, arms, and back; kneeing him in the stomach. During all of this Manny's body is very still and his voice unaffected.

> "As the person comes at you—I don't care—as they attack you somehow, I want you to really do your best to work with them; try to kind of chisel, uhm, I guess, not punish them or see them as 'you're an attacker, I'm the good guy,' but try to say he's come to you because he wants to get better, like he wants somehow… he wants somehow to understand himself better."

He's asking you to play a game of pretend. One partner plays the student and the other plays the sage. The student is approaching the sage in order to be… healed? improved? It's not clear. Whatever the answer though, the process is equated with knowing yourself. The sage works like a sculptor, chiseling away at the body with soft or hard strikes. He is looking for expressions of anxiety or fear and working to eliminate them: "try to see where you see worry." The implication here—as we have now come to expect—is that

---

[1] https://www.youtube.com/watch?v=D8IIus_paWg, accessed June 18, 2019

knowing yourself occurs through the elimination of visible expressions of fear.

Jason tries to maintain himself, coming forward as best he can. "Let them come to you; that way it's their courage that brought them forward." I can see that he's struggling, particularly when Manny challenges him with the threat of a deep strike. But Jason doesn't stop; he finds courage. Manny detects an improvement. "He's going towards the problem, and he feels solid; I'm hitting him good, and he's strong."

Over and over Jason is taken to the ground; again and again, he gets up. Manny continues, telling us all that, eventually, we'll see "a different type of peace coming over the person; he's not so worried, he starts to change somehow—he gets up like one piece." Jason stands now with a bit more confidence and relaxation.

Then, after a number of hard strikes delivered with fists and knees, Manny guides Jason down to the ground for the last time. Jason rests, breathing. Manny tells us that he needs us to perform *this* work with each other and that we'll know that we're successful when we notice a difference in the person, "you go deep into the character, deep into the personality."

Jason tries to stand but Manny stops him. "Nope." Jason tries again. "Nope." Again. "Nope."

Finally, Manny leans over and asks a question that would be awkward in another context: "Will the real Jason stand up?"

After a brief pause to take in the instruction, Jason stands with a single movement. Manny remarks, "It's already a little better."

You may recall that instructor Ryo Onishi had asserted that Systema cleanses our perceptions so that we can see things as they really are. You may also recall that I detected a realist notion of truth in that assertion. For many Systema instructors, reality is something we can access directly if we perform the right exercises. I detect a similar idea in Manny's question to Jason. The inference is that there is a real Jason buried somewhere underneath all of his worries. Systema works to uncover that buried individual, helping them to emerge in a regenerated state.

I cannot accept this. Where my instructor and others see the emergence or expression of authenticity, I see the precise opposite. I see a performance. In actuality, Manny is encouraging Jason to wear a new mask, and to step onto the stage of the world as a new persona.

Later, after having watched Manny work with Jason, and after I had reviewed the footage, I concluded that Systema is not primarily a martial art. You learn to fight, yes, but that's only a by-product of its exercises. Systema is a performance art. We play the game of student and sage, striking and wrestling and working with each other, and we call it knowing yourself. This means playing at having courage, playing at being cleansed. The goal is to one day learn our roles so well that fantasy and reality begin to blur not only for others but also for ourselves. We hope to one day *be* courageous, one day *be* clean.

***

In his seminal 1959 work, *The Presentation of Self in Everyday Life*, sociologist Irving Goffman explored the ways in which our lives amounted to elaborate performances. Compare, for instance, how you comport yourself at work and how you are at home. At work you likely dress in a different way than when you are at home, a way meant to convey a particular attitude or demeanor; you perhaps sit a little more straight; you choose your words so that they are appropriate. "To *be* a given kind of person, then, is not merely to possess the required attributes, but also to sustain the standards of conduct and appearance that one's social grouping attaches thereto."[2] What is more, when you are at work, others agree to participate in your drama; "together participants contribute to a single over-all definition of the situation which involves not so much a real agreement as to what exists but rather a real agreement as to whose claims

---

[2] Irving Goffman, *The Presentation of Self in Everyday Life* (Anchor Books, 1959): 75

concerning what issues will be temporarily honored."[3] Everyone wears "expressive equipment" such as suits and dresses, crafting their appearance and manner to fit the chosen drama, marking off their social status or indicating a temporary ritual state.[4] You theatricalize your life in nearly everything that you do, performing your chosen or assigned roles, transforming yourself into someone else from stage to stage.

You fail to notice the performance of your everyday life because you have made these dramas an integral part of your imagination, your body, and your feelings. You've learned to perform your role so well that you have come to believe in its reality. You've also learned to fear the consequences of not sufficiently and carefully attending to it.

A significant portion of yourself has its being in the opinions of others. After having distinguished between two selves—the social and the subjective—philosopher Gloria Origgi goes on to compare the social self to an animal's shell. Like a shell, your social self is part of you; it grows from you but has expressive qualities that are beyond your control, informing others' evaluations of who and what you are; it is a shell that "lives in and through others."[5] More often than not, in order to maintain your subjective integrity, your inner self, you hold this shell to yourself, identifying with it, acting how others see you and thus becoming what they say. Their dramas infect your own.

When considering how individuals evaluate the moral qualities of others, Adam Smith—famous for having theorized capitalism in the eighteenth century—often referred to a "spectator," linking moral thought to theatricality in a way which was common in the eighteenth century. However, for Smith, theatricality went deeper than mere appearances, performances, and reputations. Because he held that there was a radical and unbridgeable gap of knowledge between

---

[3] *Ibid*: 10-15
[4] *Ibid*: 24
[5] Gloria Origgi, *Reputation: What It Is and Why It Matters*, translated by Stephen Holmes (Princeton University Press, 2017): 4-13

individuals, it was impossible for you to directly perceive the feelings and experiences of another. Sympathy, to his mind, could only be achieved through imagination. If you wished to feel what another felt, you had to place yourself in their shoes, imagining yourself in their role on the stage of the world, being viewed as they would be by the world's spectators.

Furthermore, since there was no way to bridge the gap between individuals, this alternate, imaginative persona was necessarily formed from the elements of your own feelings and experiences. When sympathizing with others, you modeled—to the best of your own resources—the inner world of another. It followed then that in all those moments when you sought to understand someone else, you actually reckoned with a fiction of your own devising.[6]

A similar difficulty extended to the evaluation of your own character. You could evaluate yourself, know yourself, only by imaginatively putting on someone else's shoes, trying to simulate their judgements as if you were a spectator watching yourself.[7] From the perspective of Smith, all human sympathy and moral evaluation was, in the most important respects, a product of the dramatic imagination.

If you accept the validity of these ideas—as I do—then it becomes very difficult to take seriously any notion of human authenticity. We are theatrical animals. We wear masks in everything that we do, even when we seek self-knowledge. These masks are composed of opinions, social status, imagination, clothing, training, and habit.

Indeed, if you accept the idea that your everyday life, and even the moral evaluation of your own behavior, involves a series of related theatrical productions, then—with a little thought—you'll be led to the corollary notion that your entire life is, to an extent, composed of stories, or, at the very least, that stories play a disproportionate role in how you conduct

---

[6] David Marshall, "Adam Smith and the Theatricality of Moral Sentiments," *Critical Inquiry*, Volume 10, Number 4 (1984): 593-595
[7] *Ibid*: 598

yourself and how you evaluate your place in the world. Man, as part of being a theatrical animal, is a storytelling animal. You craft narratives about yourself and tell stories about yourself not only to arrange your experiences, but also to define who you want and ought to be. Your life story directs you toward your goals and away from your fears.[8] It is even central to how you learn. Information given to you in the form of a story is more likely to be remembered than information delivered otherwise. This is why successful teachers are the ones who use metaphors and build narrative structures around knowledge.[9]

Unfortunately, however, the same human desire for narrative which helps you to improve your knowledge can also have a subversive effect, contributing as it has to the proliferation of unwarranted conspiracy theories.[10] Psychologists have shown that knowledge acquired through storytelling has a tendency to bypass your critical faculties, shaping beliefs without your recognition. Your brain sifts through the events of the world, looking for patterns, connections, and meaning, finding them even where logic and fact might otherwise disagree.[11]

In response to this, some people may contend that stories serve merely as an escape from reality, but—if so—then they fail to admit to themselves that these 'escapes' tend to involve highly-moralized worlds of threat, passion, intrigue, death, despair, anxiety, and conflict.[12] Stories, to quote from literary scholar Marshall Gregory, "extend invitations," cueing

---

[8] Timothy D. Wilson, *Strangers to Ourselves: Discovering the Adaptive Unconscious* (Harvard University Press, 2004): 87-88
[9] Peter C. Brown, Henry L. Hoediger III, and Mark A. McDaniel, *Make It Stick: The Science of Successful Learning* (Harvard University Press, 2014): 109, 160-161
[10] For more on the distinction between warranted and unwarranted conspiracy theories, see Matthew R.X. Dentith, *The Philosophy of Conspiracy Theories* (Palgrave MacMillan, 2014)
[11] Rob Brotherton, *Suspicious Minds: Why We Believe Conspiracy Theories* (Bloomsbury Sigma, 2017): 157, 169
[12] Johnathan Gotschall, *The Storytelling Animal: How Stories Make Us Human* (Houghton Mifflin Harcourt, 2012): 49-52

your capacity for feeling, believing, and judging.[13] They help you select relevant facts, to establish meaningful relationships between facts and events, and to define positive and negative outcomes, both for yourself and for the human community writ large.[14]

Indeed, psychologists have revealed some of the ways that you unconsciously develop "parasocial relationships" with popular characters. For example, young men who enjoy stories featuring Batman and Spiderman will report feeling stronger and better about themselves after being exposed to images of their heroes.[15] Such identifications, particularly when the protagonist of the story resembles your own self-image and social group, can even influence real world behavior. For example, reading a story from the first-person perspective of someone who shares your cultural background, for instance, who—in the story—makes a point of engaging in voting will, it seems, have an influence on your own voting behavior.[16]

***

Martial arts traditions tend to transmit their core philosophical principles, the reasons behind their art, through stories, usually in a way which links the art to a larger religious ideology.[17] The histories of Judo and Yoga follow this pattern. In an earlier chapter I explained that these practices of physical culture were connected to invented traditions and popular religions. I also—to my own

---

[13] Marshall Gregory, *Shaped by Stories: The Ethical Power of Narratives* (University of Notre Dame Press, 1997): 3, 21-23
[14] Anne Harrington, *The Cure Within: A History of Mind-Body Medicine* (W. W. Norton, 2008): 21-22
[15] Ariana F. Young, Shira Gabriel, and Jordan L. Hollar, "Batman to the Rescue! The Protective Effects of Parasocial Relationships with Muscular Superheroes on Men's Body Image," *Journal of Experimental Social Psychology*, Volume 49, Issue 1 (2013)
[16] GF Kaufman and Lk Libby, "Changing Beliefs and Behaviour Through Experience-Taking," *Journal of Personal Social Psychology*, Volume 103, Number 1 (2012)
[17] George Jennings, David Brown, and Andrew C. Sparkes, "'It Can Be a Religion if You Want': Wing Chun Kung Fu as Secular Religion," *Ethnography*, Volume 11, Number 4 (2010): 543

satisfaction if no one else's—demonstrated that Systema's highly nationalistic origin story was more likely than not also an invented tradition. We saw that its origin as a way of life more probably flowed from the intersection of three modern historical currents: European physical culture, militant Russian nationalism, and a resurgent Orthodox Christian Church. Each of these traditions, in their own way, were or are concerned to overcome the threat of nervous overburden, that is, with the fast, distracting pace of modernity and its effects on the body.[18]

Systema's story, the worldview that undergirds its ethos, is the continuation of a story first told at the dawn of the second Industrial Revolution, in the nineteenth and early twentieth centuries, when locomotives, mass media, telecommunications, suffragacy, national unifications, democratic and socialist revolutions, and an all-pervasive globalization upended traditional patterns of living, both urban and rural.[19] It is a story about the corrupting influence of modernity and the need for spiritual and physical renewal.

Once upon a time humans moved naturally; they were healthy and in tune with the world around them. But now, in our modern society, stress and distraction have destroyed the ancient connection to God and nature. The practice of Systema wipes away the corruptions of modernity, cleansing you, returning you to a state of grace.

***

In an interview included at the end of *Let Every Breath...*, Ryabko—when asked about the link between breathing and spirituality—replies that:

> "The body is strengthened, purified, and prepared for prayer by proper breathing

---

[18] To better understand the concern over modernity's pace in the nineteenth century, see Stephen Kern, *The Culture of Time and Space, 1880-1918* (Harvard University Press, 1983/2003): 124-130

[19] See Jurgen Osterhammel's *The Transformation of the World: A Global History of the Nineteenth Century*, translated by Patrick Camille (Princeton University Press, 2014)

practice. The body has a natural state of strength, health, and purity, when it is ready for God's presence. The ideal blood pressure is 120/80. The ideal body temperature taken underarm is 36 degrees Celsius (96.8 degrees Fahrenheit). The ideal pulse rate is 60 beats per minute. Under stress, all these measures will rise. When these parameters are lowered, we are able to perceive God. God comes to us naturally when we feel calm, when we're asleep, or when we see the spirit realms in a coma. Breathing and prayer both help to lower these crucial physiological measures. Whereas, stress, anger, fear, resentment, etc. make our blood pressure, heart rate and temperature rise. This makes us open to the evil forces or energies, and brings destruction."[20]

Here, it seems to me, we are looking at a secularized version of a Christian story. Christianity is a moderate dualist religion; its early adherents—particularly the monastics—held that good and evil were forces in the world.[21] Men and women, were it not for having fallen to temptation, would have retained their identity with God. Now though, after succumbing to moral weakness, they must toil in a world of hostile demonic forces which threaten their physical and mental well-being.[22]

Ryabko's words evoke this ancient context, positing a duality between good and evil, material and immaterial, placing mankind at a nexus where goodness, evil, matter, and spirit mingle. At the same time, however, he also evokes a modern empiricism, speaking of precise physiological measurements. In this way, he comes to translate biometrics (pulse, heart

---

[20] Vladimir Vasiliev and Scott Meredith, *Let Every Breath...: Secrets of the Russian Breath Masters* (Systema Headquarters, 2006): 123
[21] Jeffrey Burton Russell, *Satan: The Early Christian Tradition* (Cornell University Press, 1987): 32
[22] Dale Martin, *The Corinthian Body* (Yale University Press, 1999): Ch. 1

rate, temperature) into measurements of one's access to the good and the immaterial. 'Normal' measures of pulse and heartrate reflect a body and mind that are open to the presence of God, while high measures reflect a body and mind that are vulnerable to immaterial evils.[23]

A short transcript of sayings attributed to Ryabko compiled by a student in the year 2000, very likely after the master's first trip to North America, indicates that Systema's founder did not fully enjoy his time here.

> "American society from what I have seen is very fast and stressful. Americans work long, busy days, drive in bad traffic, and try to fit too much in. No one slows down. Then you decide to exercise to relieve some of that stress, but the exercises you choose merely irritate your nervous systems further. You push and pull at weights fanatically, you race on your treadmills or stationary bicycles while you read the paper and watch the news. This only makes it worse."

Assuming that these are in fact Ryabko's true sentiments, the visiting ex-soldier found the pace of western life—its traffic and exercise regimens—damaging to the nervous system. In the next line, he even complains about modern music, speaking well only of the country music he had heard in Denver. The implication in all of this being that western life, disruptive of biometrics, obscures the presence of God. Ryabko asserts that Systema "teaches you to relax in stressful times no matter what the cause. Its life style will

---

[23] "This concept of *theosis* (or deification)—the belief that humanity's destiny is to become more like God—stands at the centre of orthodox thinking about the human person and his or her destiny." A. Edward Siecienski, *Orthodox Christianity: A Very Short Introduction* (Oxford University Press, 2019): 53

help you be a better person, which is the most important thing after all."[24]

In his *Systema Manual*, Komarov offers a similar account. He asserts that Systema's methodology, which aims for unity and wholeness of being, returns bodies and psyches to a "natural" and "healthy" state. A natural human being moves with comfort and efficiency and a healthy human being is one whose organic systems cooperate. Lacking the qualities of naturalness and health, a human being will move erratically, inefficiently, and with either too much or too little tension; the various pieces of their being will exist in opposition with one another. The practice of Systema corrects this, refining the body's movements and improving cooperation between its various organic components.

Political and social existence "clogs" the body and psyche, diminishing the qualities of naturalness and health. Laws and social pressures burden the human being with "fears, tensions, and cramps of all kinds."[25] Modernity tears the human being apart, separating the body from the external world, leaving it isolated and in conflict with itself.

> "People today are often separated from their bodies, always 'living in their heads' (in their thoughts, fantasies, or worries), and in the external world (TV, internet, etc.). For these people, the body is just an auxiliary mechanism, a means for moving around. But the body is the house of the Soul."[26]

Systema names a process of regression from the socialized human being to the newly-born, original human being—old movement and thought patterns are discarded to make room

---

[24] https://web.archive.org/web/20001214202500/http://www.russianmartialart.com/articles/excerpts.html, accessed August 30, 2019. For troubling information regarding the individual who compiled these excerpts, please also see https://johngiduckdemystified.wordpress.com/, accessed September 6, 2019

[25] Konstantin Komarov, *Systema Manual*, translated by Dimitri Trufanov (Systema Headquarters, 2014): 14

[26] *Ibid*: 151

for natural and healthy replacements which integrate the body, psyche, and soul into a coherent whole.[27]

For the most part, Komarov avoids overtly religious language in his *Systema Manual*, so it is worth taking a moment to point out that Komarov is sure to capitalize the word "Soul." He may not advertise his own faith as much as other veteran Systema instructors but it does come out from time-to-time. At the outset of the *Manual*, for instance, he refers to Systema as "the structure, based on historical Russian *spiritual* and combat traditions, of a harmonious physical, *spiritual*, and psychological training of the individual."[28] And elsewhere, he chides individuals who express "pride and arrogance" and encourages instead "spiritual openness."[29] Furthermore, in a 2011 interview, he remarks—when asked about the subject—that there are "different levels of faith. There is faith in God – that's the highest one."[30] So it seems reasonable to infer that, on some level at least, Komarov's account of modernity's effects is an echo of his mentor's.

This seems especially so when you recall that in Systema's interpretation of know yourself—influenced as it is by the theology of Russian Orthodox monasticism—being in God's presence meant maintaining an unmediated attention towards the present moment. Emotions such as pride, anger, irritation, and fear had the dual effect of disrupting the natural state of the body and introducing mediating elements into the human psyche—worries about the future or ruminations on the past. Breathing and prayer are physiological interventions and pathways back to God's presence, that is, to knowing yourself.

What we are learning here is that, for Systema's founders and veteran instructors, the process of coming to know yourself is part of a larger criticism of society and a more complex engagement with physiology. Ryabko links moral qualities to biometrics, citing stress as a spiritually disruptive

---

[27] *Ibid*: 15, 24
[28] *Ibid*: 13 (emphasis mine)
[29] *Ibid*: 230, 238
[30] http://www.russianmartialart.com/article_info.php?articles_id=53 #.XTdQmuhKjcv, accessed July 23, 2019

force, while Komarov links uncontrolled introspection and telemedia to physical and psychological disorders. Taken together, we begin to hear in faint tones a story that was given embryonic form in the late nineteenth century.

***

George M. Beard, American neurologist, famously held that the forces of industrial and social modernity—steam power, the press, the telegraph, science, and 'the mental activity of women'—had an adverse effect on the human nervous system. The ailment of modernity, which he called neurasthenia, involved a diverse array of symptoms: dyspepsia, headache, paralysis, insomnia, anesthesia, neuralgia, or sexual and menstrual irregularities.[31] But because Beard never identified a physiological basis for the disorder and because the symptomology was so vague, the causes and cures for neurasthenia ranged widely and diagnoses became commonplace; the term took off in medical literature, inspiring researchers across the world.

In late-nineteenth century Russia, after the concept had migrated from German medical literature, influential physicians such as Pavel Kovalevskii linked neurasthenia to political individualism, that is, to a lack of faith in God and a loss of national connection.[32] To his eyes, the modern Russian exhibited extreme nervousness, weakened willpower, diseased pride, and a lack of self-control. Particularly at risk, so the thinking went, were children, who would never develop a healthy nervous system if not insulated from modernity.[33]

Although enthusiasm for neurasthenic research began to wane in the 1890s, the basic notion remained popular in self-

---

[31] Laura Georing, "'Russian Nervousness': Neurasthenia and National Identity in Nineteenth-Century Russia," *Medical History* (Volume 47 (2003): 25-27
[32] *Ibid*: 37-38
[33] Susan K. Morrissey, "The Economy of Nerves: Health, Commercial Culture, and the Self in Late Imperial Russia," *Slavic Review*, Volume 69, Number 3 (2010): 654, 661; Mark Jackson, *The Age of Stress: Science and the Search for Stability* (Oxford University Press, 2013): 22-23

help books, various medical and pseudo-medical treatises, novels, and memoirs.[34] Sport clubs and publications spread across the empire, promoting physical and nervous health, linking physical fitness to social renewal.[35] The Russian Symbolist Aleksandr Blok even linked neurasthenia to anti-Semitic discourse, seeing the spread of nervousness as a result of the Jewish press.[36] Perhaps most importantly, however, the notion remained current in the medical marketplace, where, for example, cocoa and cologne were sold as a cure for agitated nerves and as a source of renewed strength and vitality.[37] In the interwar period, Americans, Europeans, and Russians continued to fixate on the damage that modernity was inflicting on their bodies, seeking cures in medicines, exercises, religion, and naturalism, even as physicians generally abandoned the idea.

Later, something called 'stress' became the bête noir of modernity. The term was coined by Hans Selye, a psychologist working out of McGill University in the 1950s. He observed that mice exposed to inhuman treatment all seemed to suffer from a similar series of ailments. He went on to infer from this that humans who expressed similar ailments did so because of their hectic, modern "stressful" lifestyle.

Contemporary physiologists saw many difficulties with Selye's research and with his wider conclusions. Nonetheless, the term gained popularity, particularly within the American military. By the 1970s, one-third of all stress researchers were attached to the military in some way. Understandably,

---

[34] Brad Campbell, "The Making of 'American': Race and Nation in Neurasthenic Discourse," *History of Psychiatry*, Volume 18, Number 2 (2007): 158

[35] *Ibid*: 671

[36] Arkadii Blumbaum, "Civilization, Irony, Neurasthenia: Anti-Semitic Discourse in the Writings of Aleksandr Blok," in *Reframing Russian Modernism*, edited by Irina Shevelenko (University of Wisconsin Press, 2018): 174-178

[37] Susan K. Morrissey, "The Economy of Nerves: Health, Commercial Culture, and the Self in Late Imperial Russia": 645-649

they were looking to explore how this new concept of stress related to the effectiveness of soldiers on the battlefield.[38]

It was in this larger context that physicians began to treat civilian stress and military stress as equivalent. Society, the pressures of our jobs, the ubiquity of our entertainments, the unheralded speed with which modern men and women experience life—it puts 'stress' on the body's energy systems, causing them to break down. Seeing the damage being done, researchers prescribed the progressive relaxation exercises designed by psychologist Edmund Jacobson, as published in his books *Progressive Relaxation* (1929) and the more popular *You Must Relax* (1934).[39] In Japan, similar exercises, such as Futaki Kenzo's "abdominal breathing method," were employed for the same purpose, albeit originally in response to diagnoses of neurasthenia.[40]

Contemporary researchers, it must be admitted, *have* linked stress to poor health and negative affect, but—as with neurasthenia—the precise connection is often poorly understood.[41] This allows for something that sociologists refer to as "stress talk." For example, in the winter of 2004, three sociologists interviewed 15 men and 14 women between the ages of 15-81 years, living in St. Petersburg, asking them about stress.[42] Nearly all of them associated the term with Russia's current economic and political situation, as well as with complex family dynamics.

What stood out to these researchers, and what is most interesting for our purposes, is that the word 'nerves' operated as a conceptual bridge, linking mental stress to physical health.[43] For these Russians the idea of stress had

---

[38] Anne Harrington, *The Cure Within*: 148-155
[39] *Ibid*: 166
[40] Yu-Chuan Wu, "A Disorder of Qi: Breathing Exercises as a Cure for Neurasthenia in Japan, 1900-1945," *Journal of the History of Medicine and Allied Sciences*, Volume 71, Number 3 (2015): 328-331
[41] Jackson, *The Age of Stress*: 15
[42] Ilkka Pietila and Marja Rytkonen, "Coping with Stress by Stress: Russian Men and Women Talking About Transition, Stress, and Health," *Social Science and Medicine*, Volume 66 (2008): 327-329
[43] *Ibid*: 332-333

taken on the qualities once contained in the idea of neurasthenia. Modernity itself was making them sick.

Whatever the name for the belief, neurasthenia or stress, there has been an ever-present reactionary current running through much of American, European, and Russian culture, which—while still valuing the convenience of technology and the progress of learning—fears modernity's disruptive influence on traditional ways of life and on natural bodies, whether human, animal, or ecological. Secularism and individualism, for a subset of such individuals, are held to be biologically disruptive, the source of disease and illness, and thus as something that needs to be cured through exercise, relaxation, breathing, and a socially conservative political program.

***

Systema's instructors frequently evoke the language of neurasthenia, particularly in their emphasis on treating nerves. Vasiliev, in an article regarding the Systema Youth Program, writes that "our respiratory system is directly connected with circulation while every blood vessel in turn is closely connected with nerve endings. Thus, breathwork has a calming, stabilizing and healing effect on the entire nervous system."[44] That same year, while answering questions about how to teach Systema, Vasiliev also wrote, in regards to slow exercises, that "the nervous system gets stronger and balanced, because there is no stress. Breath work removes the stress as soon as it arises."[45] Komarov similarly prioritizes the nervous system, writing in his *Manual* that it "plays a defining role in a person's psyche... (it) defines the individual's behavioral differences in response to physical and social stimuli."[46] Furthermore, *The Russian System Guidebook* reads that "Systema identifies fatigue – whether emotional, physical or intellectual fatigue – as its main

---

[44] http://www.russianmartialart.com/article_info.php?articles_id=45&osCsid=b4d8b353a5201e321c5c41a495c40df6#.XTnc5OhKjcs, accessed July 25, 2019
[45] https://www.russianmartialart.com/article_info.php?articles_id=40&language_id=1, accessed July 25, 2019
[46] Komarov, *Systema Manual*: 138

enemy. Fatigue has a negative effect on the whole nervous system."[47]

Systema instructors fixate on the central nervous system in a way reminiscent of Soviet medical culture at mid-century, when neurasthenia was still in play as a concept.

When trying to explain why it is difficult to "define and discuss the properly developed body," Komarov explains that "most of body development is done through manual labor, games, and acquiring professional or special skills (e.g. hunter's or warrior's)" and that bodies develop in relation to the current and future needs of their society. Men and women, he asserts, don't work hard anymore because they don't have to. And children do not play traditional games because their mothers and grandmothers are too fearful. Komarov editorializes. "People of my generation played and spent time outside with no adult supervision starting at the age of 4. Today, it is typical to see a boy of 7-9, or even older, playing under the constant watchful eye of his mother or grandmother. No traditional games to speak of!" The result of all this disruption is "a social trend today toward more feminine men and more masculine women" which threatens to carry on into future generations.[48]

It seems to me that Komarov is here suggesting a theory of degeneration, of the physical and moral decline of society due to the influence of modern technologies and mores. Bodies are not developing properly because men and women no longer have to fell trees, hunt game, or prepare meat. They no longer have to fight in wars. Once upon a time, young boys would roam free, taking into their bodies the quality of naturalness, but now, under the eyes of women, they grow feminine themselves.

What strikes me in this theory is the way that Komarov's final assessment seems to echo that of the educational theorists, demographers, and journalists who laboured in the era of

---

[47] Vladimir Vasiliev, *The Russian System Guidebook* (Kindle Edition), Chapter Six, "Introduction to the Russian Health System," Eighth Paragraph, Location 586
[48] *Ibid*: 209-210, 227-228

Leonid Brezhnev. In the 70s and 80s, they argued that Soviet policies regarding the emancipation of women had contributed to men's feminization and women's masculinization and to the decline of Russian men since the Second World War.[49] Anthropologists have noted that the myth of the primitive masculine norm has become only more popular over time. A sizable number of Russian men today see Western (i.e. modern) men as weak, and have grown increasingly concerned about the social decline of their country as a result of Western influence.[50]

Komarov recalls grappling or "sorting things out" with other children between the age of 5 and 9.[51] He comments on the courage that was required for him and other children aged 7-8 to enter into wrestling scrimmages as part of their villages' festivals or to join "celebratory crowd fist-fighting."[52] He describes playing a game involving masses of youth who would create "human walls" of 50-60 participants and then enter into mock battle with one another.[53]

Historians have noted that such carnivalesque, ritualized battles were common throughout the early modern era.[54] Indeed, violence permeated 'traditional' village lives even up into the nineteenth and early-twentieth centuries. For instance, children in the Dankov district of Riazan province would play a game called 'Wattle Fence.' In this game children locked arms in emulation of a fence. One child would then play the role of a 'firebug.' The firebug would initiate the fence's unravelling with a stick or 'match', at which point the children would chase the firebug down and beat them.[55]

---

[49] Maya Echler, *Militarizing Men: Gender, Conscription, and War in Post-Soviet Russia* (Stanford University Press, 2012): 25-26
[50] Petra Rethmann, *Russia* (University of Toronto Press, 2018): 62-70
[51] Komarov, *Systema Manual*: 72
[52] *Ibid*: 174-175
[53] Komarov, *Systema Manual*: 206-207
[54] Edward Muir, *Ritual in Early Modern Europe*, Second Edition (Cambridge University Press, 2005): 113
[55] Olga Semyonova Tian-Shanskaia, *Village Life in Late Tsarist Russia*, translated by David L. Ransel with Michael Levine (Indiana University Press, 1993): 41

So whereas before children would have engaged in ritualized violence as a rite of passage, Komarov is saying that they are now coddled, ensconced in convenience and technology. "TV, computer, and play stations have taken their toll, corrupting society...the body has become an extension of the TV, computer, and smart phones."[56] The only proper remedy for this state of affairs—outside of regular Systema practice in youth and throughout one's life—would be to return men to the world of military conscription, as in the Soviet era. Such an environment would foster natural manliness.

In an interview he remarks,

> "First, you need to look at the question of why do you need an army? It's not to defend the motherland. The army is needed so that a young person matures. So that he stops being infantile and grows up. And you have to understand this; otherwise you get a weird view of the purpose of military training. Hand-to-hand combat is needed not to solve problems, but to make a person into a *person*, in the full sense of the word...The army is just an excuse to make men go through this 'manly' training."[57]

This sentiment is echoed in the *Manual*, where we are told that "it's only the military that takes body development seriously. Out of the entire society, apparently only the military needs harmoniously developed people, so that's where physical development is still a goal."[58]

What we can take from all of this is that Systema's founders tell themselves an old story. They maintain that there is something called 'being natural' that exists outside of culture. The goal of a correct society is to foster this quality of naturalness. Towards this end, established gender norms ought to be maintained, the ritual calendar adhered to.

---

[56] *Ibid*
[57] http://www.russianmartialart.com/article_info.php?articles_id=53 #.XTdQmuhKjcv, accessed July 23, 2019
[58] Komarov, *Systema Manual*: 211

Children should be made to enact games of mimetic violence. Social technologies and innovations are antithetical to such a society. By eliminating the need for hunting and labour, they discourage family members from embracing their proper identities. Only breathing, relaxation, a pseudo-militaristic training course, and prayer can counteract these negative influences and thus maintain mankind's link to nature. A sufficiently rigorous and disciplined way of life can return men and women to the prelapsarian condition of their naturally healthy ancestors.

***

Instructors who came up under Ryabko, Vasiliev, and Komarov tell a similar story, albeit one more palatable to a North American audience, excluding discussions of gender roles or the socialization of children. We hear this story in their discussions of the concept of "power."

Glenn Murphy, having observed and trained under Vasiliev, has come to begin to believe that power

> "appears as something you can draw from the environment—real power—when you're not getting in the way yourself, where you're not blocking the transmission of power and efficiency yourself by being too tense or out of position or having bad posture and things like that."[59]

Power here is something gifted to man from the natural world, something that it transmits or hands over to us. Tension, structural deficiencies, and a bad spatial relationship each serve to disrupt this natural transmission.

Los Angeles instructor Martin Wheeler, speaking a short while afterwards, agrees but with a different emphasis. Power is a "natural state," yes, but its impediments are primarily psychological rather than physiological.

---

[59] *Systema for Life Podcast*, Episode 87, featuring Lance Rewarts and Martin Wheeler (August 16, 2019)

> "From working with Vladimir and Mikhail, I guess the one way that I see what they're, or what they're, maybe what they're—what I'm translating from what they're doing, is that you *are* powerful. And the things, the rest of your life is kinda stacking up things on top of that power so you can't feel it. And Systema's a good sort of cleansing method for removing like your fear and your ego, and, you know, and pretty well those two things; if you've covered those things then you've pretty well covered everything….Once you remove fear and ego, you start to recognize and deal with them, then you don't have to then gain power, you already are powerful underneath that. And so your natural state is power."[60]

Once the psychological obstacles of fear and ego have been removed or cleaned out, then a state of power naturally results.

Instructor Gene Smithson puts it more bluntly. After describing a quality that he names internal power, and suggesting that such power results from knowing yourself, from finding peace, and from consistently maintaining a certain character, he states that "a lot of today's culture is designed to deliberately cut you off from internal power. I don't think that internal power is an attribute that any industrial nation really appreciates."[61]

The inference here is that previous cultures, prior to the Industrial Revolution, appreciated internal power, that is, encouraged virtues such as goodness and humility, and taught how to know yourself. Modern life, we are led to think, has dis-empowered us. Indeed, in claiming that we are "deliberately" broken, he seems to also be suggesting that this has been done intentionally. Modern industrial nations,

---

[60] *Ibid*
[61] *Systema for Life Podcast*, Episode 59, Internal Power with Gene Smithson (November 16, 2018).

are "designed" to prevent the expression of goodness and humility.[62]

Manolakakis, for his part, relates a conversation that he once had with an unnamed, highly-decorated Canadian soldier. When asked about the dangers and stresses of military life, the soldier remarked on the relative ease of his life when compared to civilian life. A soldier's bad day ends in death, the end of cares, but the civilian life is not so merciful; "you guys, you die a little every day." Manny goes on from this anecdote to talk more about the modern condition.

> "All this stress is killing us, and the research has shown it's probably worse than a cigarette. Like, what is happening to our minds right now with everything that we're talking about on your phone, all the distraction on our phone, the way our mind is being played with right now, with the phones, like literally with the smart phones, constantly being gauged into some electronic device on a constant basis; we're talking about what cigarette companies are doing with our lungs—those phone companies are doing this with our brain, they're really screwing around with our brains, and our brains are the central nervous system, right? This is where the problem we're having is: we can't sleep, we can't stop thinking, we're not present."[63]

Manny goes on to state that social media has led to a perceived increase in rates of anxiety disorders among children and teenagers. He asserts that we do not yet see

---

[62] I am reminded of the comments of Susan Harding and Kathleen Stewart in "Anxieties of Influence: Theory and Therapeutic Culture in Millennial America," in *Transparency and Conspiracy: Ethnographies of Suspicion in the New World Order*, edited by Harry G. West and Todd Sanders (Duke University Press, 2003): 259-260

[63] *Systema for Life Podcast*, Episode 18, Q&A with Emmanuel Manolakakis, Part Two (January 26, 2018)

the full extent of what modern society is doing to our nervous systems.

Here Manolakakis, like his instructors, is echoing nineteenth and early-twentieth century concerns about the effects of modernity. For him, modern life is a corrosive environment, contributing to disease and the permanent impairment of children. Modernity keeps you from being present, that is, from knowing yourself.

This attitude is also evident in something Manny says earlier in the same interview. When asked about how to attain a balance between external, physical work and internal, awareness/relaxation work, Manny talks about the predominance of sight over the other bodily senses. We focus too much on what we see rather than what we hear or feel. To re-engage the other senses, we need to quiet our minds. One way to do this is to take a walk in the woods. In that space, unmarked by modern industrialism, hearing and scent return to us. This turning outward allows us—almost paradoxically—to turn inward and enter into a state of contemplation.

Another way to achieve the same effect, he goes on to say, is to attend church. Manny reports that as a boy, listening to sermons in an unintelligible Greek dialect—Manolakakis adheres to a Greek Orthodox faith—he would zone out, finding himself in a state of stillness or inner quiet. Reflecting on this latter in life, he determined that he found this stillness because the space he was in was a "real place of peace," and that he was "around good people." It was, to him, similar to being in the woods or in warm water.[64] Like Ryabko, Manny relates religious assembly, if not religion itself, to a state of nature, equating their effects on the psyche, contrasting them against the effects of the modern condition. And like Komarov, he emphasizes the damage inflicted on the human nervous system by modern technologies.

Systema's story, even among second generation instructors, seems to be that, once upon a time, mankind lived a natural

---

[64] *Systema for Life Podcast*, Episode 17, Q&A with Emmanuel Manolakakis, Part One (January 26, 2018)

existence in the presence of peace and goodness. Then, after the Industrial Revolution, that peace came to an end, and that goodness began to fade. Forces and technologies and social mores began to corrupt our minds, burdening our nervous systems, distancing us from our animal purity, robbing us of power. To return to this fabled condition, we need to return to natural ways, to prayer and to breathing.

***

If we go back now to the story which began this chapter, to Manny the sage and Jason the student, we can see the drama in its full context. The story now is one in which the student has entered the club damaged by the pace and output of modernity, its confusion of gender identities and emphasis on media technology. His body is filled with tensions, his mind with psychic wounds. Recognizing his illness, he approaches the sage, seeking to return his vision back to nature and to God. The sage strikes and manipulates the student, driving out the demons. The process is painful, but the student is brave. He stands tall and strong, taking his medicine.

Finally, the work accomplished, the student lays on the ground as if near death. It is at that moment that the sage orders him to his feet. He is reborn now, powerful and clean.

It is an interesting story.

6. Natural Movement

A typical advertisement for Systema will read:

> "*NO BELTS. NO TROPHIES. JUST SIMPLE, FULL SPECTRUM OF ACTION - FROM SOFT TO DEVASTATING.* Systema Russian Martial Art is a way of self defense and fighting that is based on the ancient Russian warrior style of combat and used in modern times by the Russian Special Operations Unit."[1]

Reading this, I am reminded of what anthropologist David E. Jones has to say about martial arts generally. Each, he asserts, engages in some combination of combat, ritual, and performance.[2] Combat can range from sport contests (as with Boxing and Brazilian Jiu Jitsu), or strikes delivered to the open air (as with popular depictions of Karate), or full-contact aggression (as with Krav Maga). Ritual can be as complex and arduous as the preparation for Sumo wrestling or as simple as a bow before stepping onto the training mats.

Performance, meanwhile, "exists where any action is done in front of an audience, even an audience of one; that is, one's self."[3] Think of the costumes of the dojo, the side-show nature of mixed martial arts, the playing of roles such as attacker and defender, the loud cries, the belts and rankings, the emphasis on visible technique.[4] These things are all, in some sense, part of an elaborate demonstration performed for others. More than this, however, they are performed for

---

[1] https://web.archive.org/web/20180831145428/http://www.systematwins.com/, accessed June 22, 2020
[2] David E. Jones, "Introduction: Toward a Definition of the Martial Arts," in *Combat, Ritual, and Performance: Anthropology of the Martial Arts*, edited by David E. Jones (Preager, 2002): xiii
[3] Deborah Klens-Bigman, "Toward a Theory of Martial Arts as Performance Art," in *Combat, Ritual, and Performance: Anthropology of the Martial Arts*: 1
[4] *Ibid*: 5-8

yourself, so that you can show to yourself that you are in fact the thing that you think you are and want to be.

Working with the distinctions between combat, ritual, and performance, we can say that Systema instructors—perhaps looking to set themselves apart in a crowded martial arts marketplace—deny in their advertisements any element of ritual and performance, emphasizing instead action and combat. They are selling a way of fighting which is ancient yet still relevant to modern war fighting.

On instructor Martin Wheeler's website, we get something more elaborate but still on-brand:

> "Subtle, brutal and uncompromising it covers all aspects of combat training from hand-to-hand to use of weapons in any and all combat enviroments (sic). With no forms or kata to memorize, no techniques, no belts, no predetermined attitudes to conform to, just natural movement that can be practiced for a lifetime. Resulting in the development of a deep understanding of human nature, Systema is truly a unique and boundless art."[5]

Here as well, Wheeler de-emphasizes ritual and performance. Systema is sold as a training method of absolute diversity, teaching students a seemingly universal fighting art. Customers don't need to learn complex, pre-set patterns of movement; they don't need to compete for distinctions; they don't need to take on any particular way of thinking or feeling about the world. They learn only "natural movement."

In light of previous chapters, which have taken up Systema's attitude and worldview, it doesn't seem true that there are "no predetermined attitudes to conform to" in Systema. But that's a different matter. In this chapter, I'd like to focus on "natural movement" so that we can begin to answer the question: what sort of martial art is Systema? Beyond the

---

[5] http://wheelersystema.com/about-systema/, accessed July 9th, 2019

advertisements, what balance of combat, ritual, and performance is it composed of?

***

Philosopher Barry Allen, writing about movement within the Asian martial arts, makes a distinction between dance movements, sport movements, and martial arts movements. Dance movements, he writes, are "endotelic," they contain their end and purpose in their own doing. You dance for the love of dance and express yourself through dance, but your dance does not exist beyond its own pre-established rhythmic occurrence. Sport movements are competitive and contesting, meant to produce affects outside of the event. You practice evading a tackle or throwing a ball for a larger purpose. "Martial arts movements are weapons, and when they are performed well, they express this design, this violent intentionality, though without any violent purpose on the performer's part;" they are "sportslike only in training and dancelike only in demonstration."[6]

When Ryabko, Vasiliev, and their students talk about natural movement, they are—beyond denying ritual and performance—attempting to further distinguish Systema from traditional martial arts. A Systema instructor's demonstrations appear to be dancelike in that they exist to express an idea or an image. However, anyone who has had the pleasure of working with a skilled master will tell you that such demonstrations can leave traces of their occurrence, deepening your understanding of the event, preparing your body for further, deeper work.[7] Systema's movements can express intentionality, violent or otherwise, but they are never *designed* to take any specific form.

In its martial arts movements, the art aims at ease and efficiency, at comfortably and spontaneously produced results, done with proportionality and sensitivity to the surrounding context. Ideally, nothing is designed and nothing

---

[6] Barry Allen, *Striking Beauty: A Philosophical Look at the Asian Martial Arts* (Columbia University Press, 2015): 135-141
[7] On traces, see Löic Wacquant, *Body and Soul: Notebooks of an Apprentice Boxer* (Oxford University Press, 2006): 59

is complicated. Ryabko, in his *Instructor Seminar* video, uses the example of buttering bread. Traditional martial arts may get the bread buttered but why do it in such an exaggerated manner? Just butter the bread like a regular person.[8]

This is in sharp contrast to other martial arts where everything is designed and engineered to produce specific results under agreed-upon conditions. In MMA, for instance, the primary—if not sole—means of learning is through rote memorization. Thought or contemplative reflection on techniques is reportedly frowned upon during training sessions. Fighters are encouraged rather to embody their strategy and tactics through the endless repetition of drills.[9] To pick an example, should a fighter be set to face a strong wrestler with excellent takedowns, he or she will likely drill their sprawl and practice correct timing for a well-placed knee. These drills make fight-winning skills a habit so that they can be accessed and delivered more quickly, automatically, even in fatigue.

Systema's instructors also want to teach their students how to respond automatically to an attack but they come at the goal by other means. Their thinking—right or wrong—is that the body is a complex adaptive system, capable of making split-second decisions when faced with stimuli. If attacked, a body knows more-or-less what to do. However, because people are generally fearful of contact or because their bodies have stiffened up over time or because they are not comfortable going to the ground, many freeze up or make poor decisions when faced with conflict. They thrust their hands forward in fright at an oncoming car or worry too much about getting hurt to confront a bully.

In order to free the body for decision-making, Systema instructors work to get students comfortable with contact, comfortable with rolls, comfortable with moving from the line of an attack. That way, when the body makes a decision, it

---

[8] Mikhail Ryabko, *Instructor Seminar* (Russian Martial Art, 2018)
[9] Dale Spencer, "Habit(us), Body Technique and Body Callusing: An Ethnography of Mixed Martial Arts," *Body & Society*, Volume 15, Number 4 (2009): 127-129

can execute that decision without the impediment of fear and discomfort, defending itself automatically.

Part of this process involves learning how to stay calm, moving quickly from a state of excitation to something approaching relaxation. As Konstantin Komarov puts it, "the basis of Systema practice is a calm psyche, expressed and maintained with minimal, precise movements."[10]

Los Angeles instructor Menamy Mitanes describes well the difference between this approach and the approach of other martial arts. He admits that some martial arts practice meditation and train to be calm,

> "but a lot of them they sort of do it separately, you know? You go into meditation, you know, being quiet and so forth, but when you fight, you fight. But in Systema—like yoga too: yoga you sit and meditate but when you get up and do things, you know, how much yoga do you have? But in Systema, we try to do it in action, we try to be calm; that's what we focus on anyway, right? We try to relax, breathe, and, you know, we pay attention to those. So I think that's the unique part of Systema training."[11]

When both the mind and the body are comfortable and calm, even when faced with difficulties or dangers, a human being can take appropriate actions without making things more complex than required.

This leads us to something else which distinguishes Systema practitioners: we practice being gentle and vulnerable. This is in sharp contrast to combat sports where fighters engage in body-callusing exercises "whereby the fighter takes his/her body as a site of action and aggressively seeks, through the incorporation of body techniques...to harden the body and

---

[10] Konstantin Komarov, *Systema Manual*, translated by Dimitri Trufanov (Systema Headquarters, 2014): 17
[11] *Systema for Life Podcast*, Episode 84, featuring Menamy Mitanes (July 5, 2019)

turn it into a weapon."[12] Systema engages in a number of exercises that are painful, yes, but they are better thought of as massage. The goal is not to harden the body but to soften it.

A tree is strong at its core, rooted in the ground, yet it sways in the wind. Paradoxically, this allows it to retain its strength. Similarly, if you throw a rock at a glass window, it shatters. But if you throw that same rock at some sand, the force of the impact dissipates with a thud. Systema instructors believe that a hardened body is like a tree that does not sway or sand which has transformed into glass: it breaks rather than bends.

Besides, Systema's students aren't training to fight other humans in a cage. And even if they were, how often do such contests occur? It seems to me, as it does to many Systema practitioners, that your concern should not be that you'll one day suddenly fall through a trap door and find yourself required to battle it out in the gladiatorial arena of a generic supervillain. Your concern ought to be road rage. Or a petty robber. Or that someday you might come across a friend, family-member, or acquaintance who, due to either chronic or acute mental illness, has lost control and turned violent. You don't need a kimura in those situations. You need to be tactful, observant, and humane.

This method of training, which de-emphasizes fighting techniques in favour of normal-looking, instinctual responses to danger and the elimination of heightened tension and emotion, does have its admittable downside. Glenn Murphy, in conversation during an interview, remarks that

> "it's almost like we go straight in, at the top end, with principles, right? The things that we're thinking about are not, like, let's learn to punch and kick, or let's learn to grapple and later let's see if we can learn how to align with gravity and be heavier or align with gravity that you deliver a heavier strike

---

[12] Dale Spencer, "Habit(us), Body Technique and Body Callusing: An Ethnography of Mixed Martial Arts": 126

or something like that, right? And some people kind of have alluded to the fact that if you don't have the context, the fighting context, to hang those ideas off that it might be that you flail around for a while, right? If you don't really know how to—a basic framework of how to strike or how to grapple in the first place, you might not be able to fully appreciate what Systema has to offer."[13]

However, I don't think that this "go straight in" approach is so much a bug in Systema's program as a feature of it. Ryabko, in *Systema Wrestling*, is quite open about the fact that his teachings are meant to serve as a basis for sport training. You first learn how to breathe and how to move with fluidity and *then*, if you want, you can learn submissions, walking and crawling before running.[14]

Komarov more or less concedes the point in his *Systema Manual*. "The elements of Systema, wrestling on the floor, for example, *are tools for methodical learning, which is different from combat applications.*"[15] Having described a drill in which a student, sitting on the ground, "escapes attack without becoming agitated, holding the breath, or getting stuck in a dead-end position, but moving constantly and with minimum effort," he insists that it isn't worth spending much time on such drills since "such work can easily be interpreted as a combat application, which confuses students and distracts them from developing their body and psyche."[16]

For Komarov, learning Systema and learning to fight are related but nonetheless distinct activities. To illustrate this, he describes a situation in which he was faced with a student trying to show what a knife attack looks like "on the street."

---

[13] *Systema for Life Podcast*, Episode 84, featuring Menamy Mitanes (July 5, 2019)
[14] Mikhail Ryabko, *Systema Wrestling* (Russian Martial Art, 2005)
[15] Komarov, *Systema Manual*: 40 (emphasis in original)
[16] *Ibid*: 42-43

Without fanfare, Komarov sprayed water in the man's face and disarmed him in the moment of disorientation.

The majority of Systema practice is what Komarov terms "methodical learning," and any martial arts-related activities or weapons are merely tools for such learning. Combat ability is something else that is learned afterwards.[17]

I am a terrible striker. My form is really poor. This is largely due to never having sought instruction outside of Systema. It's not something that interests me. Yes, I can hit. I've even begun to be able to strike with depth and direction and precision. But people with boxing backgrounds tend to mop the floor with me during sparring. And anyone with training in wrestling or BJJ is likely to grind me into the ground and submit me. This is the same for the majority of people that I train with.

Generally speaking, in my opinion, Systema does not make great fighters. It makes people who can take a punch, who can handle pain above the normal everyday threshold, who can stay calm and alert in chaos, and who—one hopes—can act appropriately to escape or nullify dangers when they erupt.

***

In a previous chapter, when speaking about Systema's narrative core, we encountered the word 'power.' Power is one of Systema's "somatic codes." Somatic codes are words or phrases that are "meaningless to the beginner, but become gradually loaded with significance....as the student's understanding of them is modified through somatic experience."[18] When the goal is to develop a feeling for something rather than to offer empirical descriptions, the

---

[17] *Ibid*: 40-41
[18] Einat Bar-On Cohen, "*Kime* and the Moving Body: Somatic Codes in Japanese Martial Arts," *Body & Society*, Volume 12, Number 4 (2006): 75

tendency is to impart learning and take instruction using simple words and phrases.[19]

If you listen long enough to veteran instructors, words like 'power' will pop up over and over again. *Light, heavy, full, clean*: these are some of Systema's fundamental somatic codes. They are words that mean nothing to you when you first start training but become common sense after you've played the game long enough.

Let's see if I can help you understand what 'light' means in Systema. Or, at any rate, what 'light' means to me after having trained for as long as I have. Light is the feeling, bodily and emotional, that you gain when you've established "natural body position." Stand up for a moment and follow these instructions:

1) Raise your shoulders up towards your ears and then roll them back so that your chest sticks out a slight bit more than normal;
2) Starting the movement from your knees, march softly in place, making no sounds;
3) Tuck your bum in slightly to eliminate or lessen the curve in your lower back;
4) Relax your hips and neck;
5) Be sure to feel the floor under your feet and the air that surrounds every inch of your body.

If you've done this, you might feel lighter, like your lungs and organs are floating inside you. This is an approximation of the feeling of *being light*.

From my perspective, this is where the sensory-motor core of Systema begins, from this feeling of lightness and relaxation. The goal is to retain that feeling even when presented with opposition and tension, even when in uncomfortable positions, even when it's been a long day. The

---

[19] Doris McIlwain and John Sutton, "Yoga from the Mat Up: How Words Alight on Bodies," *Educational Philosophy and Theory*, Volume 46, Number 6 (2014): 9-12

reality, of course (at least in my case), never matches the ideal. Nonetheless, lightness is the perennial goal.

Natural body position and lightness are two interrelated parts of Systema's martial arts strategy. People who are light are normal looking. They haven't taken a stance to indicate that they are ready to fight. They don't communicate aggression. Vasiliev explains the value of this:

> "If I come to you looking like I'm ready to fight, with my shoulders tense and my fists raised, you can prepare yourself. But if I come normally, nothing special, with my posture relaxed, breathing calm, facial expression neutral, etc., then I can easily hit you anywhere, quickly and powerfully."[20]

Systema teaches you to be light so that you could—if it were ever required—devastate an unsuspecting opponent. It's a defense mechanism in that no one wants to attack a happy person and an offensive advantage in that no one expects a happy person to bust your teeth.

Students, having attained lightness, then work to be heavy and full. Heaviness is a dual quality. On the one hand, it is the product of bodies that have been strengthened through calisthenics, through tumbling, push-ups, squats, and the like. On the other hand, it is a product of learning how to relax and let gravity perform its work.

Because of its dual origin, it seems to me that heaviness tends to emerge in Systema from wrestling. Over time, you learn to become like a wet blanket, draped over someone, not to smother them (although you can) but to keep them down. Eventually, you transfer that feeling from groundwork to standing, letting it add power to your kicks and strikes. The solidity of character and feeling of security which emerges from this in turn produces a greater feeling of calmness and comfort.

---

[20] Scott Meredith and Vladimir Vasiliev: *Strikes: Body Meets Soul* (Russian Martial Art, 2015): 73

Fullness is something beyond the feelings which result from heaviness. What distinguishes the two things—heaviness and fullness—is that whereas heaviness is a physical state which produces an emotional one, fullness is an emotional state which manifests itself physically.

Komarov, in his part of the *Excellence Seminar* video, offers an illustrative exercise. With a partner, you should first try to strike with a simulated feeling of anger. Second, you should try with a simulated feeling of neutrality. Finally, you should try with a simulated feeling of love. Striking with love, with that quality of feeling and action, is fullness.[21]

In class, Manny explains how the feeling should begin as if you had placed a sphere in your chest. It should prevent you from deflating but not feel like a pressure. Rather, it should feel like an overflowing of happiness inside you. In this way, you begin to transition from comfort to kindness.

Associated with all of these feelings is the word clean. "Clean work" is work that is performed without forethought or undue emotional influence. The phrase expresses that an action has been taken as an instinctual response rather than as a conscious tactic, without fear, pride, or anger, without tension.

There are a few things to note from all of this. The first thing is that each of these qualities—being light, heavy, full, and clean—are products of relaxation. Relaxation is the key attribute of a Systema practitioner and the highest order goal of all its exercises.

The second thing is that, as we have already alluded, this emphasis on relaxation and its attendant qualities is part of a larger martial arts strategy, informing its approach to wrestling and striking. Through relaxation, you learn how to respond appropriately to violence; through relaxation, you slip past the defenses of your opponent; through relaxation, you marshal the power of gravity during your attack. Each of these somatic qualities intertwine with one another. They are

---

[21] Konstantin Komarov, *Excellence Seminar: Inner Control* (Russian Martial Art, 2010)

meant to produce in the individual practitioner a totalized bodily and emotional conversion experience. Moving from tension and fear to being light, then from lightness to being heavy, and then from heaviness to being full, and then, finally, to being clean inside, the person who begins the process does not fully resemble the one who emerges at the other end.

***

Writing about the Israeli Survival School of Ju Jutsu, Einat Bar-On Cohen explores how martial arts clubs "attempt to mold and divert violence from its natural course... formalizing it," imbuing violence with meaning and sense.[22] Students of the Israeli Survival School, for instance, wear gi and ranked belts, bowing before entering their training space. At the beginning or at the end of each class, they engage in a ceremonial reflection on the foundation of Israel, the sacrifices and massacres of the past, and the threats of the present-day. Through such an act, the violence of the proceedings is directed towards nationalistic ends, towards the practitioners' memories, imaginings, or experiences of genocide, colonialism, and terror. Within this dramatic context, students wear guards for their teeth, groins, and knees, engage in rapid and constant movement, and disarm knives and pistols, all in "an atmosphere of permanent emergency."[23]

Similarly, Israeli Krav Maga clubs, citing the threat of domestic and international terrorism, frequently place students into situations that evoke feelings of fear, helplessness, and constriction, steadily increasing the intensity of the moment by introducing new, awkward, and impossible situations, teaching students to display their aggression and direct it against their attacker—to fight rather

---

[22] Einat Bar-On Cohen, "Survival, an Isreali *Ju Jutsu* School of Martial Arts: Violence, Body, Practice, and the National," *Ethnography*, Volume 10, Number 2 (2009): 156
[23] *Ibid*: 160-161

than freeze or flee.[24] The Israeli military's counter-terror training program likewise exposes soldiers to fear work (*sfiga* or 'absorbing'), striking recruits repeatedly in the stomach and face. It then teaches *teleifa* or 'attacking,' that is, how to access naked animal aggression so as to make it second nature.[25] Violence is placed into the context of nation and domestic terror, revealed to be part of a zero-sum view of biological life. Get them or they will get you. Or, if they prevail, take them with you.

Systema, as one would imagine, is generally opposed to the above approach. Where Krav Maga and other modern counterterror training methods teach students how to access mindless, uncompromising aggression when presented with uncomfortable, painful, or violent threats, Systema teaches students how to access relaxation. Relaxation slows or halts the mind, freeing the body to make appropriate decisions in the moment.

Yet despite this opposition, or rather, through this opposition, Systema—like Krav Maga and other martial arts—nonetheless orients its practices in the direction of a nationalist ideology. Ryabko, when asked about the use of kindness as a self-defense technique, remarks that

> "any approach to life and martial arts that does not destroy a person's body, soul, family or nation is a correct approach.
>
> What many martial arts provoke in people is pride, ego, cruelty, and aggression. The world is not very kind. It destroys a person's soul.
>
> Pride destroys a person. Anything that destroys a person's soul is not good.

---

[24] Einat Bar-On Cohen, "Globalization of the War on Violence: Israeli Close-Combat Krav Maga and Sudden Alterations in Intensity," *Social Anthropology*, Volume 18, Number 3 (2010): 271-275
[25] Limor Samimian-Darash, "Rebuilding the Body Through Violence and Control," *Ethnography*, Volume 14, Number 1 (2012): 58

Negative emotions are not correct. Look at the biomechanics of other martial arts. Some destroy the body of a person. If you constantly deliver strikes against hard objects you destroy your joints. You get arthritis. This type of training destroys a person's body. He has constant pain in his joints. If a person is irritated and nervous he is no good for his family or country."[26]

The first thing to note in all of this is that, for Ryabko, the goal of life itself, not to mention martial arts training, is to maintain a functioning national unit. This should not surprise us given the art's place within Russia's nationalist tradition. Nevertheless, it is worth a comment, particularly since Ryabko seems to idealize the family, treating it as a subunit of the nation. In Systema, a healthy family (one imagines he would say 'nuclear family') is constitutive of a healthy nation. Such social conservativism is a common element of nationalist ideology.

The second thing to note is that Ryabko views the majority of martial arts as antithetical to his higher order nationalist goals. Why? Because they foster negative emotions and damage bodies. This in turn results in irritation and nervousness. Here, even in the realm of martial arts, we are dealing with a response to modern society's effects on emotions and nerves.

Systema substitutes relaxation for aggression in its martial arts training with the same end in mind as Krav Maga, that is, the preservation of the nation, but it does so, we could say, from the bottom up, with a more generalized strategy, one focused on maintaining the existing social fabric rather than on vanquishing external threats. For Systema, the most pressing danger to the nation is not terrorism—although such forces of 'evil' certainly exist in the estimation of Systema's founders—but rather bodily and emotional disorder.

---

[26]https://web.archive.org/web/20160314103019/http://members.aikidojournal.com/private/interview-with-mikhail-ryabko/, accessed June 22, 2020

***

Critics may claim that Systema's emphasis on relaxation disqualifies it as an effective martial art. In a world of hard knocks, surely an approach which prizes violent, animalistic aggression and a never-ever-quit attitude is what's required. Criminals and terrorists are animals; why shouldn't we be animals too?

This is the mindset of self-defense gurus such as Rory Miller. In his *Meditations on Violence*, Miller claims that: "You are not you. Who you think you are, the story you tell yourself every day, is an illusion."[27] In order to truly engage with violence, you need to break your "identity story" so that you can adapt to the situation at hand.[28] We hear something similar from Tim Larkin in his *When Violence is the Answer*: "violence is a tool, not a moral proposition."[29] His opinion is that traditional martial arts habits such as blocking, countering, and "using energy" to redirect attacks are useless. We ought instead to step through an opponent with each strike, thinking like a predator, desiring to injure first and fastest.[30] Our goal should be "targets," which he defines as anatomical structures "that can be crushed, ruptured, broken, or otherwise rendered useless, thereby rendering your opponent useless."[31]

The first reason for not harnessing aggression in this manner is the most obvious. Ryabko is right to say that such approaches are damaging, both physically and psychologically. For example, interviews with participants of the *Lochama Ba'Terror* reveal that many experienced post-traumatic symptoms and regret having relinquished elements

---

[27] Rory Miller, *Meditations on Violence: A Comparison of Martial Arts Training and Real World Violence* (YMAA Publication Centre, 2008): 41
[28] *Ibid*: 72
[29] Tim Larkin, *When Violence Is The Answer: Learning How to Do What It Takes When Your Life Is At Stake* (Little, Brown and Company, 2017): 66
[30] *Ibid*: 85
[31] *Ibid*: 148

of their humanity to a larger war machine.[32] But, beyond the psychological toll, there is another less obvious reason for de-emphasizing aggression in training. This is that even militaristic courses *designed to produce actual killers* face the same conundrum that all approaches to violence face: how do you train for something that potentially results in disability, disfigurement, or death without yourself suffering these fates? How do you 'make it real' without making it real?

The Israeli Army runs a course for Close Combat Instructors. A rite of passage in this course is the 'Fights' session—two hours of continuous one-on-one combat, wherein participants in the centre of the ring fight each other in ten second shifts, each participant cycling in and out of the event, changing only when they quit, fall down, or are injured. Participants wear protective gear and are not allowed to strike genitals or eyes; past that, anything goes. Observing this event and interviewing the participants before and after, Cohen discusses the 'Fights' virtual nature. Yes, the participants are engaged in an endurance contest of aggression and contact which resembles the chaos of combat in wartime, but we are still dealing in this instance with a controlled and staged event, bracketed off from the flow of real life. The goal of the event is not to engage with violence as such but rather to train the body and mind in a particular ethic, a particular valuation of masculinity and aggression.[33] Otherwise there would be no protective gear. And thus no 'Fights'. Violence would destroy the entire event.

The 'Fights' session is a performance meant above all to transform individuals into instructors, so that they move and feel and believe that they are seasoned combatants, persons who have gone through hell and came out the other side ready for more.

---

[32] Limor Samimian-Darash, "Rebuilding the Body Through Violence and Control": 52-58
[33] Einat Bar-On Cohen, "Once We Put Our Helmets On, There are No More Friends: The 'Fights' Session in the Israeli Army Course for Close-Combat Instructors," *Armed Forces & Society*, Volume 37, Number 3 (2011): 521-525

Systema, which does not employ gloves or padding in its training, faces the same dilemma concerning violence, albeit with the added difficulty of including breath and relaxation training. Metanes, in the same interview cited earlier, comments that

> "in Systema, you still get hit, get kicked, get submitted—we can't lose that because you still have to experience certain dangers, as close to, let's say, reality as possible. It's not reality, because you're training, however, you can sort of go close to it, simulate it without being damaged. That's what Systema training provides."[34]

The key words here are "without being damaged." Systema's founders and veteran instructors recognize the reality of violence as much any other "real world" approach to the subject. But they try to balance the needs of that subject with the priorities of their larger drama and narrative. Systema works to teach students how to engage with violence from the position of the sage, from the position of natural body posture, from the position of one seeking national strength and familial unity. And it does all of this in opposition to what it perceives as the corrosive forces of modernity.

***

Let's take some time to go into class and think more about the ways that Systema, through its martial arts practice, through its engagement with violence, embodies its larger dramatic and narrative core. How do Systema's participants perform their martial art?

First of all, there is no standard Systema class. Each class provides students with the opportunity to practice breathing, improve bodily sensitivity, learn to move freely, and train to overcome the resistance of other bodies. But you never know in what combination or in what way. One aspect of the class will focus on, for example, moving through crowds, while

---

[34] *Systema for Life Podcast*, Episode 84, featuring Menamy Mitanes (July 5, 2019)

another might introduce working from a sitting position, or on disarming knives or sticks.

That said, more often than not, a typical class will begin with a mixture of breathing exercises and calisthenics. In my own experience, the instructor might invite students—perhaps between 15 or 20 men and women, many wearing their branded t-shirts—to lay comfortably on their backs, arms and legs slightly spread. Calling out instructions, he or she might direct us to take a moment to inhale and exhale without tension, telling us that we should feel like air is coming in and going out without assistance. Then, after having spent some time breathing comfortably, we might be asked to inhale as deeply as possible, using maximal tension, and then be directed to exhale as quickly as possible, in one short burst. Eventually, this process might be inverted, so that the inhale is as quick as possible and the exhale as long as possible.

Assuming that this is how a class began, such a series of exercises might only last for five to ten minutes. However, practiced over many years, these inspiratory and expiratory exercises are likely to increase lung volume, diaphragm thickness, and exercise capacity, even if not practiced with as much intensity as in clinical experiments.[35] This is particularly so if we perform them while walking and then while running.

These sorts of breath-centred exercises are likely also to improve self-awareness, helping us to learn what it feels like to breathe with and without tension. Komarov, in his *Systema Manual*, writes that the ultimate goal is to learn how "to inhale completely without tensing the body."[36] Even if this

---

[35] Stephanie J Enright, Viswanath B Unnithan, Clare Heward, Louise Withnall, and David H Davies, "Effect of High-Intensity Inspiratory Muscle Training on Lung Volumes, Diaphragm Thickness, and Exercise Capacity in Subjects Who Are Healthy," *Physical Therapy*, Volume 86, Issue 3 (2006): 349-350; Stephanie J. Enright and Viswanath B. Unnithan, "Effect of Inspiratory Muscle Training Intensities on Pulmonary Function and Work Capacity in People Who Are Healthy: A Randomized Control Trial," *Physical Therapy*, Volume 91, Issue 6 (2011): 900
[36] Komarov, *Systema Manual*: 20

goal is merely aspirational, there are many advantages to having a conscious awareness of your own breathing, especially in situations which threaten to become anaerobic, such as in wrestling or sparring.

From here we might move into a series of slowly performed body weight exercises. As Komarov explains in his *Manual*, for the muscle knots that "function sub-optimally, limiting the movement and the ability of the muscle to flex and extend" we ought to struggle through slow push-ups, squats, and leg-raises. Slow exercises force the body to go through those knotted areas.

You can feel this for yourself. Most people will do a push-up very quickly. But when forced to slow down, taking 10-20 seconds to elevate and the same amount of time to descend, 'blank spots' appear where the body does not have full control of the muscles and where tension creates bumps in the movement. Spending time in these stiff areas, making good use of full-body breathing, you re-connect the muscles to the brain and, in Komarov's estimation, allow accumulated tensions to dissipate. Since this is hard work, it often evokes negative thoughts and feelings. Early on in your training, you'll want to quit. For Komarov this is a positive sign, one that means that the stored energies are "leaving the body."[37]

Having practiced slow exercises, we might then transition into movement drills. What is interesting about movement in the context of Systema, beyond what has already been said about its probable origins in late nineteenth-century Europe, is how much the art's concept of bodily freedom resembles the expressionistic dance of Rudolf von Laban.

In his *The Mastery of Movement on the Stage* (1950), the highly influential dance theorist distinguished between free and bound movements, that is, between movements which originated in the trunk of the body and those that emerged from a static trunk.[38] Free movements are the bedrock of Systema's martial arts practice. Manny will often lead the

---

[37] Komarov, *Systema Manual*: 179-180
[38] Rudolf Laban, *The Mastery of Movement*, 2nd edition, translated by Lisa Ullman (MacDonald & Evans, 1960): 21

class through a sequence of joint rotations beginning from the head, progressing downward from the shoulders to elbows, from the wrists to hands, and then finally from chest to hips, before combining each element into a roiling ocean of free bodily expression. At other times, he might even have us stand on a single leg so that we can explore balance and the limits of the unburdened leg, training to take action from a single point of support.

We might then move on to partner work. This would allow us the opportunity to blend these Laban-esque movements with emotional training. For example, with our partner, we might go back-and-forth trying to apply and escape headlocks. One partner attempts the headlock, the other escapes with their movement, and—during their escape—initiates the next headlock, so that the process become fluid, dancelike, and circular.

Such an exercise requires trunk-initiated movement and the maintenance of posture under restriction and pressure. After all, it is one thing to practice free movement without impediment; retaining that attitude when someone has their forearm at your neck is an entirely different proposition.

Manny often encourages his students to enter into a state of controlled chaos in which bodies entangle and the line between attack and defense blurs to the point of near unrecognizability. In this state, from this feeling, beyond the comprehension of reason, the body itself takes over, learning how to gather the relevant information "to constrain the perception-action coupling so as to respond in a timely fashion," so that it can protect itself through movement without thought.[39]

Thomas Fuchs and Sabine Koch, therapists working out of the University of Heidelberg, offer a helpful way of describing the emotional work involved in such drills. Citing earlier researchers, they posit that there are four basic emotional

---

[39] John Sutton, "Batting, Habit and Memory: The Embodied Mind and the Nature of Skill," *Sport in Society*, Volume 10, Issue 5 (2007): 770

movements "related to the gestures of giving, getting, removing and escaping":

- moving oneself 'toward the other' (e.g., affection, mourning),
- moving the other 'toward oneself' (e.g., desire, greed),
- moving the other 'away from oneself' (e.g., disgust, anger), and
- moving oneself 'away from the other' (e.g., fear).

Such movements, they go on to claim, are connected to bodily senses of "expansion or contraction, relaxation or tension, openness or constriction, etc." In anger, we expand outward to push away; in love, we relax and open ourselves.[40] Putting aside whether or not these descriptions are true to emotional reality generally, they appear to me true in the context of Systema.

I can tell you that escaping a headlock is an emotional experience. There are feelings of pride, since you don't want to get caught in the headlock; there are feelings of irritation and pain resulting from forearms grinding against your ears, neck, face, and jaw; and there are, for many, feelings of fear: stuck in a headlock is a bad place to find yourself. Using Fuchs and Koch's categories of emotional movement, we can say that the tendency with headlocks is to want to move the other away or to move the self away from the other.

The challenge that Systema offers its students is to overcome the movements of anger and fear so that you can embrace the movements of affection and care, moving towards the other like the sage who wishes to heal. With this in mind, Manny talks about feeling "what your partner needs" in any given moment. Yes, escape from the headlock, but make sure that you are "with them" as you do so, feeling their tensions and bodily restrictions and going "towards them"

---

[40] Thomas Fuchs and Sabine C Koch, "Embodied Affectivity: On Moving and Being Moved," *Frontiers in Psychology*, Volume 5, Article 508 (2014): 4

while you work, helping them to relax and to move with greater and greater freedom.

All of Systema's martial arts exercises, if you choose to practice them with the intended purpose, aim in this direction. Each is a training in free expression and in moving forwards with relaxation and fullness. This is so even when the exercise takes a combative turn, as with wrestling, takedowns, or disarmaments.

***

Although Systema has largely eliminated formal ritual from its practice, there is nonetheless one ritualistic act which caps off the end of each class: the circle.

The ritual of circle is meant to serve as an opportunity for students to confess their challenges or attest to their progress. *The Russian System Guidebook* explains that, during circle, "each person should explain what he understood, what he's having trouble grasping and what insights he might have had during class."[41] In reality, however, participants, sitting side-by-side, legs crossed or holding their knees to their chests, tend only to use circle time to complement the instructor for the class and for the instructor to broadcast, in this silent moment, the day's moral lesson.

This is perhaps just as well.

Systema, like the majority of martial arts, is an intimate practice. Martial artists, to borrow a term from anthropologist Jérôme Beauchez, engage in an "agonistic collaboration." Through partner work, each participant is involved in a "shared management of the confrontation" wherein they strengthen their bodily techniques while achieving greater mastery of their emotions.[42]

---

[41] Vladimir Vasiliev, *The Russian System Guidebook* (Kindle Edition)
[42] Jérôme Beauchez, "Embodying Combat: How Boxers Make Sense of Their 'Conversations of Gestures'," *Ethnography*, Volume 20, Issue 4 (2019): 9-10

We've all shown up and put in the work. Staging the drama of Systema can be arduous and challenging. For the past hour and a half, we've been moving and breathing, absorbing strikes and wrestling, wielding training weapons and looking inward. We're tired now. Contented or troubled, depending on how we think our performance went.

Once each has had their opportunity to speak, and after the instructor has had their say, we back-roll out of the circle in unison, symbolically disbanding the unit, adjourning the session, closing the curtain.

There is chatting at this time, laughter and farewells. People cleaning themselves of sweat.

We leave relaxed, feeling simultaneously a little lighter and a little heavier, and—hopefully—a little more at peace with the world than when we arrived.

7. Courage

Manolakakis speaks to a group of fourteen participants in a seminar held sometime in the summer of 2011.[1] One of the goals of the seminar is to learn how to feel normal under strain. Manny informs his students that "base knowledge should never go past normal." To explain this, he uses the analogy of a pyramid. If your total skill-set were a pyramid, then the base of that pyramid would be composed of the full breadth of your skills as performed with a feeling of normalcy.

And what is this feeling? Normal is the feeling of getting out of bed or putting on your shirt or walking down the street. Training should aim to establish in the student a large base of skills that can be performed with a normalcy akin to everyday life. This allows the student to increase the intensity of their output without worrying about their structure collapsing.

If you want to run a marathon, first see if you can walk a marathon; then see if you can jog a marathon—acclimate your body to the task and then slowly increase the intensity.

Earlier, to acquire a sense of what normal feels like, Manny had students walk around the room and perform simple exercises. Now, having captured that feeling of regularity, he works with the group to expand the pyramid's base. Manny begins to lightly and rhythmically punch a long-time student named Mark.

> "I'm gonna walk around Mark in a normal way, what I deem normal, in the same fashion, and strike—slowly around him, normally, and the person needs to feel okay with taking this stuff on them, otherwise he's

---

[1] Sadly, in this instance, I was not in attendance. Video footage can be found here:
https://www.youtube.com/watch?v=H2gelFfCJCg, accessed July 22, 2019

just full of nerves, right? Again we're talking about building a 'warrior's spirit', a warrior's mentality; it doesn't worry about these little hits, he's already—it's to strengthen him, so that he's not freaking out upon contact, okay?"

Manny says this while striking Mark in the stomach, face, chest, and elsewhere. At the same time, Mark moves around slowly, walking and raising himself up and down from the ground, maintaining his own normal while Manny follows and continues to speak.

> "Release yourself from the burden of being hit—your body is totally free; it can deal with anything that happens; it doesn't matter, the body starts to learn how to deal with it at all levels, right? And then your ability goes into your head, being able to take in information, offensive applications. Really guys, in a full blown fight, no one's thinking defense; it's all offense."

Komarov expresses a similar idea in his *Systema Manual*, where we read that, through taking strikes, "we deal with fear, calm the psyche, and liberate our hands for doing the work, so that they strike and grab, instead of protecting the body."[2] And Vasiliev, in *Strikes: Soul Meets Body*, remarks that "in a fistfight, you have to know that people can hit you too, you accept that, that's the first decision. But when fear disappears, pain will disappear too. When you're not afraid anymore, there won't be that much pain. Fear of pain is worse. Plus people have fear based on ego, not wanting to lose face."[3] What Systema aims to impart on its practitioners is a habit of feeling normal even under painful or otherwise intense conditions. Doing so eliminates worries, leaving the person with an increased sense of freedom.

---

[2] Konstantin Komarov, *Systema Manual*, translated by Dimitri Trufanov (Systema Headquarters, 2014): 50-51
[3] Scott Meredith and Vladimir Vasiliev: *Strikes: Body Meets Soul* (Russian Martial Art, 2015): 61

Having undergone this training at greater and greater intensities over a long period of time, you can begin to feel confident in your body's autonomy, to trust that you will not over-react to injury, that you can put aside pain, fear, and anger in order to deal intelligently with an immediate problem, such as a fight or an assault. By exposing you to pain and other excitations, and then conditioning you to relax automatically, instructors give you the means to behave with courage.

***

Philosopher Daniel Putman distinguishes between three sorts of courage. Physical courage involves overcoming the fear of death or bodily harm; moral courage, overcoming the fear of social ostracism or rejection; and psychological courage, overcoming psychological distress itself. You overcome these threats—physical, moral, psychological—for the sake of a goal, which itself might be physical, moral, or psychological. You might have to face pain and fear in order to protect yourself or a family member; you might have to face harassment in the workplace in order to renounce a dangerous or harmful practice; you might have to face fear itself in order to eliminate or come to terms with it.[4]

The courageous person acts to overcome fear for the right reasons, moving toward a correct goal. They stand up for themselves for a reason with an ethical goal in mind; they speak out for a reason; they grapple with moral quandaries for a reason.[5]

In a Stoic framework, the reasons and ethical goals for such actions revolve around the concept of inner freedom, that is, the goal of having the courage to relinquish that which is not up to you and to cling to that which is. In an existentialist framework, on the other hand, the reasons and ethical goals revolve around eliminating willful or systematic ignorance

---

[4] Daniel Putman, "The Philosophical Roots of the Concept of Courage," in *The Psychology of Courage: Modern Research on an Ancient Virtue*, edited by Cynthia L. S. Pury and Shane J. Lopez (American Psychological Association, 2010): 10
[5] *Ibid*: 12

and the bad faith rationalizations which underpin much of our daily conduct.[6]

Systema, in my experience, is an excellent vehicle for exploring and developing physical, moral, and psychological courage within a Stoic framework. As a martial art, it contributes to physical courage by, in the words of philosopher Simone Roberts-Thomson, "providing us with situations in which to act courageously, by engendering self-control in us, and by helping us to understand that some things are not to be feared."[7] Working with a knife, particularly a real knife, will show you precisely how dangerous and versatile a weapon it can be. Being struck in the face and stomach will show you both how bad a fight can get and also how much of the danger is the product of the popular imagination. Willfully holding your breath until the point of panic, or even the point of breaking, will reveal a previously unknown realm of psychological conflict, showing you just how hard it is to overcome yourself. The ultimate goal of such Stoic training is to experience, as historian Miira Tuominen puts it, "not emotions or passions, but proper feelings (*eupatheia*) that involve true attributions of value and no excessive physiological reactions such as growing pale connected with fear."[8]

What the practice of Systema does not do, what it leaves its students to do on their own, is to develop courage within an existentialist framework. To the Stoic, the good life is one spent acting, feeling, and thinking in a proper manner. It is a framework of correct personal, internal responses.[9] Justice, however, names a responsibility for the actions of the community. We are social creatures, embedded in history. Nothing in Systema itself prepares you to engage with that fact. For example, it doesn't give you the opportunity to

---

[6] *Ibid*: 14-19
[7] Simone Roberts-Thomson, "The Promise and the Perils of Martial Arts," in *Philosophy and the Martial Arts: Engagement*, edited by Graham Priest and Damon Young (Routledge, 2014): 21
[8] Miira Tuominen, *The Ancient Commentators on Plato and Aristotle* (University of California Press, 2009): 257
[9] For common criticisms of the Stoic position regarding well-being, see Heather Battaly, *Virtue* (Polity, 2015): 138-140

forego racism or bigotry; it doesn't give you any tools that are useful to the analysis of the origins of economic inequalities; it doesn't provide critical insight into the ongoing colonial project we call late capitalism. The implication of Systema's Stoic framework is that those issues do not belong to your person and are thus beyond your control; you should stop criticizing others and focus on your own faults. Indeed, Systema's nationalist and conservative ideology, it seems to me, actively militates against just this sort of existentialist philosophical consideration.

Again, none of this is to say that Systema practitioners cannot, if they so choose, explore these themes. But doing slow push-ups doesn't reveal anything useful about history. Learning how to wrestle doesn't provide the context for facing gaps in your knowledge, willful or otherwise. Natural movement, in itself, doesn't allow you to enter into a space of criticism.

What I'm saying is that believing that these activities—exercise, combat, or movement—will somehow return you to a harmonious state of nature in which you are purified of the corruptions of modernity, this will only make it more difficult for you to express existential courage. When you believe with certainty that there is a way that things *are and always will be*, then you'll never quite be able to move past that. An entire realm of courage may be closed off to you.

***

Komarov, at the opening of his *Systema Manual*, explains that what separates Systema from other martial arts is that it is "primarily a holistic approach to the individual, considering the interconnected unity of body and psyche, as well as the inseparable unity of peace (daily life) and war (extraordinary situations)." Because of this interconnectedness and inseparability, a body "cannot change piece by piece – only as a whole."[10] Later in the book he defines the psyche as "the complex human characteristics of active reflection of the environment resulting in self-

---

[10] Komarov, *Systema Manual*: 13-14

regulation of the person's behavioral activities," which—Komarov goes on to assert—derive from the nervous system, "an integral system of interconnected nervous cells, tissues, and organs, which controls all other systems in an organism and regulates the body's responses to internal and external stimuli."[11]

Here Komarov is evoking a view of the human body that did not exist prior to the dawn of the twentieth century. It wasn't until then that physiologist Walter Cannon, through the use of newly developed X-ray technology, traditional methods of surgical intervention, and the measurement of blood and stomach pressure, reached the conclusion that pain activated the central nervous system, halting the body's regular course of action, shifting energies to circulation, respiration, and musculature, mobilizing it for high-intensity struggle. The goal of such whole-body disruptions, he argued, was to maintain what he called homeostasis. The body, fragile yet adaptive, coordinated the actions of "the brain and nerves, the heart, lungs, kidneys and spleen" so that the internal environment of the body reflected, to the extent possible, the needs and demands of the external environment.[12]

After silently evoking homeostasis, Komarov supplements his account with concepts borrowed from another late-nineteenth and early-twentieth century physiologist. Citing Ivan Pavlov, he asserts that the inherent properties of the human nervous system include strength (ability to function normally under heavy load), mobility (ability to switch quickly between excitation and relaxation), and stability (the

---

[11] *Ibid*: 138
[12] Stephanos Geroulanos and Todd Meyers, *The Human Body in the Age of Catastrophe: Brittleness, Integration, Science, and the Great War* (The University of Chicago Press, 2018): 146-156

balanced expression of excitation and relaxation).[13] Komarov then lists the nervous system's two acquired properties: "personal character" and "accumulated tension."

Character is defined as "a means to hide or display psychological activity" and as "certain habitual behaviors in response to excitation/relaxation of the nervous system." Accumulated tension, meanwhile, provokes "the excitation of the psyche."[14] Elsewhere in the book, he describes accumulated tensions as fears that "stay in the body as tensions and tights areas" and fears that are "present in the head as high-activity areas in the brain."[15]

There are four things that interest me in all of this. The first thing, as I've already alluded, is that none of Komarov's model of human nature predates the nineteenth century. In this way, his writings are consistent with my larger contention that Systema is a way of life formulated in the modern era.

The second thing, and this is another reason to bring up Cannon and Pavlov, is that for Komarov, you are, as a body, nothing more than your central nervous system. It is the fundamental root of your being, the coordinator of your body and the source of your mind. As a consequence, any meaningful project of self-development would need to improve the strength, mobility, and stability of your nervous system, to increase its capacity to operate under strenuous conditions and to shift down from over-excitation and avoid under-excitation.

The third thing, which relates to the second, is that your central nervous system is an accumulator, receiving, storing,

---

[13] The use of Pavlov should not surprise us. Official Soviet documents announced that "'the principles of Pavlov's theory of the nervous system are fundamental to the formation of motor habits, the physical qualities of strength, speed, stamina and skill, improving the functional capacity of the organism – especially for the purposes of work.'" Quoted in James Riordan's *Sport in Soviet Society: Development of Sport and Physical Education in Russia and the USSR* (Cambridge University Press, 1980): 55-56
[14] Komarov, *Systema Manual*: 138, 142
[15] *Ibid*: 170

and releasing energies. Character is an expression of the strategies and tactics which allow your body to successfully receive and release nervous energies. Your personality, your various ticks and routines, represent your central nervous system's way of successfully maintaining homeostasis. Accumulated tensions, on the other hand, represent moments when your nervous system found itself unable to adapt to the excitements of its environment. These surplus excitations—with nowhere else to go—were deposited into your musculature and other organs. The goal of training is to clear out storage while developing a nervous system that receives and releases energies without remainder.

A fourth thing which follows from this is that Komarov, in a way that perhaps he himself would not recognize, describes a body that is profoundly neurotic. In a sentence that would not be out of place in psychoanalysis, Komarov writes that,

> "In the process of maturing and accepting the norms and laws of a society, the modern person ventures very far from his/her natural and healthy state, typically present only in early childhood. This 'departure' has to do with the clogging of the body and psyche—fears, tensions, and cramps of all kinds. For only through a system of bans and limitations, enforced by fear of punishment, does the average person get prepared for life within a society. We tend to live like this, stumbling through life 'skewed'."[16]

Offering a fairly basic theory of repression, Komarov tells the story of how society, through pain and fear, grafts acquired properties—character and accumulated tension—onto the pristine inherent properties of the central nervous system. He goes on elsewhere to explain that "our thoughts and behaviours are fear-based."

Fear "helps us hold on [to society] by limiting our desires and demands in order to please others."[17] The body remembers

---

[16] *Ibid*: 14
[17] *Ibid*: 170

serious physical injuries, creating protective areas of tension around them. Similarly, Komarov asserts, the mind—due to evolutionary pressures—creates barriers to action in order to avoid censure; "the emotion of shame was to curb behaviors that go against social norms, which could risk the person's survival (long ago, being banished and becoming an outlaw meant death)."[18]

This aspect of Komarov's thought, it seems to me, is correct in many ways. Philosopher Judith Butler remarks that the subjection of the individual by society "must be traced in the peculiar turning of a subject against itself that takes place in acts of self-reproach, conscience, and melancholia that work in tandem with processes of social regulation."[19] This is to say that we become members of society by taking society's norms and procedures into our bodies as fear and sadness, acting as if people are watching and judging even when they are not. Indeed this is perhaps why threats to social status activate the same areas of the brain as do physical pain and why those who—due to some combination of environment and inheritance—are resistant to such socio-neurological conditioning tend to veer towards criminality.[20]

Systema, as "a method for overcoming fear," is from this perspective a method of curing neuroses and freeing one from the restraints of shame.[21] It is for this reason that, if you were to ask him for a definition of a courageous individual, Komarov might describe such a person as someone who maintains a nervous system with strong inherent properties, is capable of dealing efficiently with high and sustained levels of excitation, and possesses very flat, almost non-existent acquired properties. A courageous person, in other words, would have little in the way of ticks

---

[18] *Ibid*: 171-172
[19] Judith Butler, *The Psychic Life of Power: Theories of Subjection* (Stanford University Press, 1997): 18-19
[20] On threats to social status in the brain, see Jeff Wise, *Extreme Fear: The Science of Your Mind in Danger* (St. Martin's Griffin, 2011): 94; on neurological makeup and criminality, see Adrian Raine, *The Anatomy of Violence: The Biological Roots of Crime* (Vintage, 2014): 115-119
[21] Komarov, *Systema Manual*: 180

and gestures and would accumulate the least amount of tension possible.

***

When Komarov leads students through an exploration of pain, he is—in his mind—leading them through an exploration of the very foundations of awareness and thought itself. In a recorded seminar, Komarov describes, with the assistance of an interpreter, the role of pain in childhood development.

> "Because the pain pre-dates the person's awareness, because the pain was already there when the little child—the small, small kid—was even able to think consciously. And the person gets familiar with the world around them through pain. You bumped into something or you grabbed a lightbulb that is hot or a stove; it's always the pain signal that you receive. So pain is the foundation of our awareness and the foundation of our thinking process."[22]

Providing a definition that accords perfectly with early twentieth century physiology, Komarov asks and answers: "What is pain? Again, it's a sharp nervous excitation. So, in addition to the pain, you have emotions: anger, feeling desire for revenge, you name it."[23]

Systema practitioners use pain as an emotional trigger, seeking to destabilize their bodies in controlled environments, setting in motion a host of physiological reactions that need to be brought back under control.

Today, pain researchers have produced a "biopsychosocial" model which posits that

---

[22] Konstantin Komarov, *Excellence Seminar: Internal Control* (Russian Martial Art, 2010)
[23] *Ibid*. On the role of pain as a trigger for fear and rage, see Geroulanos and Meyers, *The Human Body in the Age of Catastrophe*: 151-152

"the experience of pain is determined by the interaction among biological, psychological (which include cognition, affect, behavior), and social factors (which include the social and cultural contexts that influence a person's perception of and response to physical signs and symptoms)."[24]

This is to say that pain describes "a manner of feeling."[25] This manner is composed of autonomic bodily responses such as nerves firing; psychological responses such as feeling irritated or focusing on the cause of injury; and socialized responses such as when a cold item feels hot because you expect it to feel that way or if it is coloured red rather than blue.[26] Your reaction to pain is also strongly influenced by your disposition. If you are generally optimistic, enthusiastic, and hold yourself in good esteem, you are less likely to catastrophize during the experience of pain than someone lacking those qualities.[27]

Beyond the individual, there are also larger cultural and political responses to pain. For example, although at first glance liberal societies tend to take a dim view of the matter, it is instead the case that they relegate pain to distinct spheres. In obstetrics, some women choose natural child birth over anaesthetized. In sexuality, some persons choose to incorporate sadomasochistic behaviours. In the gym,

---

[24] Gordon J.G. Asmundson and Kristi Wright, "Biopsychosocial Approaches to Pain," in *Pain: Psychological Perspectives*, edited by Thomas Kadjistavropoulos and Kenneth D. Craig (Lawrence Erlbaum Associates, 2004): 42
[25] Joanna Bourke, *The Story of Pain: From Prayer to Painkillers* (Oxford University Press, 2014): 7
[26] G. Lorimer Mosely and David S. Butler, "Fifteen Years of Explaining Pain – The Past, Present, and Future," *Journal of Pain*, Volume 16, Number 9 (2015): 10
[27] Suzanne M. Skevington and Victoria L. Mason, "Social Influences on Individual Differences in Responding to Pain," in *Pain: Psychological Perspectives*: 185-188; J.H. Lee, S.K. Nam, A-R Kim, B. Kim, M.Y. Lee, S.M. Lee, "Resilience: A Meta-Analytic Approach," *Journal of Counseling & Development*, Volume 91, Number 3 (2013): 269-274

persons adhere to the adage of "no pain, no gain." All of this is either condoned or celebrated. As anthropologist Talal Asad remarks, "modern hostility is not simply to pain, it is to pain that does not accord with a particular conception of human being—and that is therefore in excess."[28] Liberal societies value sensations of pain to the extent that they allow for the consensual expression and development of individual identities. Pains beyond that threshold are to be eliminated or lessened.

With this biopsychosocial model in mind, psychologists have developed a number of reliable pain interventions. They are designed to allow you to take greater control over your experience: patterned breathing, burst breathing, progressive muscle relaxation, and movement and awareness training.[29] Systema employs all of these techniques. What perhaps sets the Russian Martial Art apart from other pain interventions is its method of training the nervous system itself.

***

Komarov identifies two means of working with the central nervous system. The first is through the body and the second is through the psyche itself. Working with the body involves dealing with pains and nervous excitations while lying on the ground, sitting, walking, moving, and in crowds. Psyche work, on the other hand, involves the mastery of breathing, the training of bodily sensitivity, the exploration of fear, and the management of peak levels of stress and emotion.[30]

For an example of body work, let's return to Fight Club's 2011 Summer Seminar. Manny sits on the ground, his legs straight in front of him. He's speaking to the group as a student steps on the inside of his left leg.

---

[28] Talal Asad, *Formations of the Secular: Christianity, Islam, Modernity* (Stanford University Press, 2003): 122
[29] Stephen Bruehl and Ok Yung Chung, "Psychological Interventions for Acute Pain," in *Pain: Psychological Perspectives*: 246-252
[30] Komarov, *Systema Manual*: 145-146

"Right away the muscles start to contract. I can feel the nerve now down the femoral artery, and for me all my breathing effort is to relax this because I know any more from this will be worse for me...So as he steps I relax more...I let the pain come to my head, but not my nerves."[31]

Manny describes a physiological process. The first responses to pain are simultaneously muscle contraction and nerve firing. The body tenses up to protect the threatened area and the nervous system sends signals to the brain ordering the body to struggle away from the source of the disruption. Systema instructors teach students to stay with this sensation, to find calmness under duress, not initiating a feedback loop. The tendency is to overly focus on the pain, which in turn increases its perceived intensity. Systema's initial strategy in such situations is to use quick, powerful breathing bursts to get control of pain and then afterwards to use relaxation and steady breathing to prevent the pain from overtaking the body as a whole, keeping it localized.

An article written by Vermont instructor Mark Kutolowski describes how he used this method to manage the pain of an accidental foot injury. In an earlier class at Systema HQ in which he had hurt his neck, Vasiliev had told Kutolowski: "You now have a choice as to how far you let this penetrate and spread into your psyche." Further told to keep moving and breathing, Kutolowski was given time to manage his response. Later then, during his more serious injury, he remembered to keep breathing, to repeat the Jesus Prayer, and to localize the tension to his foot, not letting the pain disrupt the rest of his abilities.[32]

Since pain reactions are products of the autonomic nervous system, in order to manage them successfully, you need to train the psyche like a muscle, tensing and relaxing it,

---

[31]https://www.youtube.com/watch?v=H2gelFfCJCg, accessed August. 12, 2019
[32]https://www.facebook.com/notes/systema-vasiliev-russian-martial-art/pain-and-freedom/2578188325565026/, accessed August 12th, 2019

thereby improving the nervous system's inherent properties. To this end, Komarov asserts that stresses given to the body must be fast, abrupt, and strong.[33] Like a nail through your foot.

A whip is excellent for this sort of work. Anyone who has worked with this tool in training can tell you that, after a moment's delay, the pain radiates outward from the point of contact, inspiring an immediate state of agitation. Komarov explains that in such a state the torso stiffens, often in the stomach; breathing stops, and then the body is activated—faster heart rate, higher blood pressure, altered breathing, sweats, and muscle tensions.[34] The goal, once you've entered into this sudden state, is to stay with the pain, using breathing and movement to calm the nervous system, working towards a return to normal relaxation.

Another way of activating this response in the nervous system is through voluntary breath holds. Komarov instructs students to lay on the floor, to exhale calmly without tension in their chest or diaphragm, and then to hold their breath for as long as possible.[35] Having myself spent a good amount of time with this drill, I can say that—sadly—it doesn't take long to feel like you are reaching a breaking point, particularly if you attempt to practice with any sort of elevated physiological state; research shows that this can shorten breath holds by as much as half.[36] As your lungs slowly begin to decrease in volume, signals are sent to the brain, inducing a state of panic; your body begins to think that it is in some sort of trouble. For me, waves of tension radiate outward from the stomach, making me feel like I have to go to the washroom.

If you are patient and let your body move in the way that it wants to, then you can ride this wave to a period of peaceful silence. Eventually, however, that silence will end and another wave will come. And another. And another. Until you

---

[33] Komarov, *Systema Manual*: 156
[34] *Ibid*: 167
[35] *Ibid*: 156
[36] Mike Parkes, "Breath-Holding and its Breakpoint," *Experimental Physiology*, Volume 91 (2006): 4

finally let yourself breathe. At this moment, as part of the recovery, you ought to engage in burst breathing, short and rapid inhales and exhales performed in as relaxed a manner as possible. Such breathing, according to Komarov, should take 50% longer than the breath hold, slowly shifting down to regular full-body inhales and exhales. You will know that you have recovered sufficiently when you are "overtaken by a state of emptiness, with no thoughts, desire to breathe, or do anything." You feel heavy and relaxed, as your body leaves voluntary tension behind.[37]

***

With enough practice recovering from the effects of pain and fear, a student can come also to recognize in themselves their own unique biopsychosocial reactions to pain and duress. This in turn allows a student the opportunity to preemptively mitigate any ill effects. Self-awareness training and breath-centred attention can also help with this.

One means of developing self-awareness is to habitually divide your attention between the outside world and your own inner state. Komarov suggests a regimen of near-hourly body scans. Taking roughly a minute to scan and relax your body on a regular basis, he claims, will "after a month or so," permanently split your attention, instilling a rudimentary bodily sensitivity.[38]

Manny, with his usual flare for metaphor, often reminds his students to "check their gauges" while they work. Establishing an analogy between a race car and the human body, he remarks that he often sees people ignoring their body's "speedometer and tachometer while training." To correct this mistake, he suggests a series of exercises, to be conducted with appropriate breathing, performed with steadily decreasing amounts of tension: full, half, and quarter. He suggests then taking this bodily feeling, the sense of working at less than full capacity, and applying it to

---

[37] Komarov, *Systema Manual*: 156-157
[38] *Ibid*: 151

partner work, to dealing with strikes, kicks, and takedowns.[39]

The end goal of all of this work with breathing and bodily attention is to develop the skill of unconsciously shifting breath automatically "as needed, when under physical or psychological stress including strikes, falls, pain, fear, aggression, lifting weights or any other intensive workout."[40] Through your conscious efforts, your body learns to make adjustments in breathing automatically to meet its oxygen needs, allowing it to remain normal under duress.

Researchers, looking at the distinction between concentrative or "top-down" attention coming from the conscious mind and receptive or "bottom-up" attention coming from the bodily unconsciousness, have described the transition from concentrative to receptive attention like a skill shift, a move from novice to expert.[41] In this research they have even associated actual physiological changes in the brain with such a shift.[42]

Like novice meditators, Systema students first lessen the intensity of pain by breath-capture and isolation. Then, over time, as their body incorporates the skill of concentrative attention and shifts towards receptive attention, they learn to experience "lower emotional reactivity to stimuli aimed at evoking regulation strategies," that is, they actually feel less pain and anxiety and come to no longer need to regularly employ the physiological strategies of pain management.[43]

---

[39] http://norcalsystema.com/tips/tip3.html, accessed August 14, 2019
[40] Komarov, *Systema Manual*: 148
[41] Alberto Chiesa, Alessandro Serretti, and Janus Christian Jakobse, "Mindfulness: Top-Down or Bottom-Up Emotion Regulation Strategy," *Clinical Psychology Review*, Volume 33, Issue 1 (2013): 92-93
[42] Amishi Jha, Jason Krompinger, Michael Baime, "Mindfulness Training Modifies Subsystems of Attention," *Cognitive, Affective, & Behavioral Neuroscience*, Volume 7, Issue 2 (2007): 110
[43] *Ibid*: 88; Zella E. Moore, "Mindfulness, Emotion Regulation, and Performance," in *Mindfulness and Performance*, edited by Amy L. Baltzell (Cambridge University Press, 2016): 34-36, 41-42

***

As Rory Miller tells us in *Meditations on Violence*, self-defense is about "recovery from stupidity or bad luck, from finding yourself in a position you would have given almost anything to prevent... The critical element is to overcome the shock and surprise so you can act... Self-defense is about *recovery*."[44] Speaking about the relationship between exercising for fitness and exercising for self-defense, he also asserts that self-defense "is largely about dealing with surprise and fear and pain, none of which is useful in developing fitness."[45]

If this is true, and it does appear to be true, then Systema is an excellent way of training for self-defense. Working with pain and fear with the intent of improving the central nervous system's capacity to take on work and to recover automatically from over-excitation, it teaches students how to return to a calm and cognizant state of mind during emergencies. Furthermore, it does so through combat-like training, which prepares bodies to wrestle, deliver strikes, and disarm weapons.

At the same time, it increases the student's sense of freedom and happiness, teaching them—through exercises of courage—that pain can be a gift; we can use it to practice being "good at suffering."[46]

---

[44] Rory Miller, *Meditations on Violence: A Comparison of Martial Arts Training and Real World Violence* (YMAA Publication Centre, 2008): 9
[45] *Ibid*: 10
[46] Joanna Bourke, *The Story of Pain:* 105-119

Conclusion

Was my extended mediation on Systema foolish? Did I learn anything from writing this book? Yes.

On the one hand, researching for and writing (and re-writing) this book focused me. I came to class each time with a purpose. I knew where I was and where I wanted to go. I knew that I had to live up to my own words as best I could or risk losing credibility. The result, in my opinion, was an improvement in my practice.

On the other hand, this project involved *a lot* of reading. The time spent hunched over books, wrestling with words, taking notes, typing at a computer, it brought tensions into my life that I could probably have done without. Worse, there were many times when my deep emersion into the history and ideology of Systema led me, ironically, to a state of aggravation and disaffection.

But I don't regret any of it. This book showed me where my personal limits with Systema are. I know now precisely how far I'm willing to go into its worldview and discourse. I've said the things that have been burning within me. Liberated now from this burden, I hope to return to my practice with a clean slate.

This does not mean, however, that I won't have more things to say in the future. I have decades of training ahead of me. Perhaps in that time I'll discover a new perspective and wish to share it. I wouldn't be surprised.

I am writing this conclusion several months into the COVID-19 pandemic, when many (if they were lucky) were forced to work from home and childcare centres had been closed. The time crunch of job and child forced me to abandon two almost-finished chapters. The first regarded the relation between freedom and *habitus* in the practice of Systema.[1] The second would have dealt with the themes of intuition, pride, humility, and wisdom. Many thoughts and ideas ended up on the cutting room floor. When time permits, I'm certain that these 'lost' chapters will be completed.

Indeed, reviewing the material, I'm surprised by the vast number of topics that I'd failed to touch on and by the questions that remain to be asked about Systema. There is so much more to say.

My sincere hope is that this book spurs others with greater skills and resources than myself to finish what I began, that others with academic training and wider language proficiencies will work to confirm or deny my many speculations and inferences. Most of all, I hope that I have inspired someone to produce complete biographies of Systema's founders.

Systema is a way of life with a complex history. The basic structure of its practice and ideology stems in many ways from a tradition begun in ancient times when philosophy was an act of attention, meditation, and 'the care of the self' aimed at self-transformation, when knowing yourself meant taking on the characteristics of a wiseman.

At the same time, as I hope that I have successfully demonstrated, Systema's proximate cause, the moment from which it was born, was very modern.

As a way of life, Systema resulted from the mixture of state propaganda, militarization, popular religion, and a eugenic impulse. The founders of the art, swept up in all of these currents, crafted with their personalities, skills, and hard work a regimen of practice designed to cure, through breathing, movement, and suffering, the destructive neuroses of modernity.

---

[1] For an introduction to the concept of *habitus* as it relates to martial arts, see Loïc Wacquant, *Body & Soul: Notebooks of an Apprentice Boxer* (Oxford University Press, 2004)

Someone passionately devoted to the orthodoxy of Systema may not agree with the substance of this argument as I've presented it but I nonetheless hope that such a person would understand where it comes from.

Whatever your opinion, please know that throughout the process of writing this book, I tried above all to be fair to the source material while remaining honest with myself.

Acknowledgements

First and most of all, I want to thank my instructor Emmanuel Manolakakis for his patience and open-mindedness. He has been a great teacher to me and more than a little bit of a role model.

Beyond that immediate debt, I want to thank Mikhail Ryabko, Vladimir Vasiliev, and Konstantin Komarov for giving me a puzzle that will busy me the rest of my life.

To find a certified Systema club in your area, use the Russian Martial Art School Locator.[1]

Thanks also goes to my fellow students at Fight Club for their camaraderie and support. In particular, I'd like to thank Mark Fan and Jason Smith. The former for being the best of us and the latter for the many late night chats.

Christopher Levesque gets a special mention for his elegant front cover design.

Special mention also to Glenn Murphy. Although we've never really properly met, he has nonetheless enriched my understanding of Systema and helped to make this book possible.

Finally, thank you to my wife Cynthia for putting up with my interminable research projects. You're a beautiful woman and a great sport.

---

[1] https://www.russianmartialart.com/schoollocator.php

About the Author

James Sommerville has been practicing Systema since 2006. He has a PhD in History from Queen's University, specializing in the theory and practice of the dictum 'know yourself' in the Italian Renaissance.

Printed in Great Britain
by Amazon